SMP 11-16

Book R2

The right of the
University of Cambridge
to print and sell
all manner of books
was granted by
Henry VIII in 1534.
The University has printed
and published continuously
since 1584.

Cambridge University Press

Cambridge
New York   Port Chester
Melbourne   Sydney

Published by the Press Syndicate of the University of Cambridge
The Pitt Building, Trumpington Street, Cambridge CB2 1RP
40 West 20th Street, New York, NY 10011, USA
10 Stamford Road, Oakleigh, Melbourne 3166, Australia

First published 1986
Fifth printing 1989

Illustrations by Chris Evans and David Parkins
Diagrams and phototypesetting by Parkway Group, London and
Abingdon, and Gecko Limited, Bicester, Oxon.
Cover photograph by John Ling

Printed in Great Britain at the University Press, Cambridge

British Library cataloguing in publication data
SMP 11–16 red series.
  Bk R2
  1. Mathematics – 1961–
  I. School mathematics Project
  510   QA39.2
ISBN 0521 31455 0

Acknowledgements
The authors and the publishers would like to thank Ordnance
Survey for permission to reproduce the map on page 114 (Crown
copyright reserved)

Contents

1 Using a calculator

A Order of operations

Look at this calculation: $2 + 5 \times 3 =$

There are no **brackets**, so it can mean two different things.

It could mean $(2 + 5) \times 3 =$, which comes to 21,

or it could mean $2 + (5 \times 3) =$, which comes to 17.

What happens if you do it on a calculator, like this?

$$\boxed{2}\ \boxed{+}\ \boxed{5}\ \boxed{\times}\ \boxed{3}\ \boxed{=}$$

The answer depends on the type of calculator you have, because there are two different types of calculator.

The first type we shall call the 'left-to-right' (LTR) type, because it works through the calculation from left to right, like this:

$2 + 5$ {That's 7 so far.} $\times 3$ {That's 21.} $=$ {Result 21}

The second type of calculator automatically puts brackets round any multiplications or divisions, and does them first.

If you key in $2 + 5 \times 3 =$, it will do $2 + (5 \times 3)$, and get 17.

We shall call this type the MDF type ('multiplication and division first').

A1 Key in $2 + 5 \times 3$ on your calculator.
Which type, LTR or MDF, do you have?

A2 Write down what answer you think you will get when you key this into your calculator:

$$8 - 3 \times 2 + 6 \div 2 =$$

Now do it on your calculator and check that you were right.

A3 Write down the answer you think you will get from your calculator for each of these. Then check each one.

(a) $4 \times 7 - 2 \times 5 =$ (b) $10 - 6 \div 2 =$

(c) $18 - 10 \div 2 - 5 =$ (d) $9 - 2 \times 4 + 5 =$

(e) $12 \div 3 + 6 \div 2 =$ (f) $14 - 2 - 10 \div 2 =$

B Calculations with brackets (1)

If your calculator has brackets keys, then calculations with brackets in them are easy.

If it does not have brackets keys, you have to think carefully when you have a calculation with brackets in it.

Here are some examples done on each different kind of calculator without brackets keys.

(1) LTR type without brackets keys

$8 \times (4 + 3)$ Do $4 + 3$ first, then multiply the result by 8.

| 4 | + | 3 | × | 8 | = |

$(9 + 7) \div 4$ Brackets can be ignored here.

| 9 | + | 7 | ÷ | 4 | = |

$5 + (8 \div 2)$ Do $8 \div 2$ first, then add 5 to the result.

| 8 | ÷ | 2 | + | 5 | = |

(2) MDF type without brackets keys

$8 \times (4 + 3)$ Do $4 + 3$ first. Press $=$. Then multiply by 8.

| 4 | + | 3 | = | × | 8 | = |

$(9 + 7) \div 4$ Do $9 + 7$ first. Press $=$. Then divide by 4.

| 9 | + | 7 | = | ÷ | 4 | = |

$5 + (8 \div 2)$ Brackets will be inserted round $8 \div 2$ automatically.

| 5 | + | 8 | ÷ | 2 | = |

Questions B1 and B2 are intended for people whose calculators do not have brackets keys.

If your calculator does have brackets keys, try doing the questions without using the brackets keys.

B1 Do these on your calculator. Then do them in your head and check that your calculator method was right.

(a) $4 \times (3 + 2)$ (b) $6 \times (3 + 1)$ (c) $3 + (8 \div 4)$

(d) $(3 + 7) \times 2$ (e) $(5 + 7) \div 3$ (f) $10 + (3 \times 2)$

B2 Do these on your calculator.

(a) $18 \cdot 3 + (4 \cdot 2 \times 1 \cdot 5)$ (b) $6 \cdot 5 \times (2 \cdot 7 + 3 \cdot 9)$ (c) $15 \cdot 8 + (10 \cdot 2 \div 1 \cdot 5)$

(d) $(7 \cdot 3 + 1 \cdot 8) \times 2 \cdot 4$ (e) $(10 \cdot 4 - 2 \cdot 6) \div 1 \cdot 3$ (f) $2 \cdot 7 \times (3 \cdot 8 - 1 \cdot 3)$

Now check your answers. The correct answers are at the bottom of page 5.

C Calculations with brackets (2)

The 'horizontal bar' sign for division acts like brackets in a calculation.

For example,

$$3 + \frac{8}{2} \quad \text{means} \quad 3 + (8 \div 2) \qquad \frac{10}{3+2} \quad \text{means} \quad 10 \div (3 + 2)$$

C1 Do these on your calculator.

(a) $12\cdot8 + \dfrac{15\cdot6}{1\cdot6}$ (b) $\dfrac{12\cdot8 + 15\cdot6}{1\cdot6}$ (c) $\dfrac{12\cdot8}{1\cdot6} + 15\cdot6$

(d) $11\cdot2 + \dfrac{8\cdot4}{1\cdot4}$ (e) $\dfrac{11\cdot2}{1\cdot4} - 8\cdot4$ (f) $\dfrac{11\cdot2 - 8\cdot4}{1\cdot4}$

Look at this calculation: $\dfrac{779}{18 + 23}$.

It means the same as $779 \div (18 + 23)$.

If you have brackets keys, the calculation is easy.

If you do not have brackets keys, there are two things you can do.

(1) Do $18 + 23 =$. Make a note of the result. Then do $779 \div$ ⟨the result.⟩

(2) Use the calculator's **memory** if it has one. (The memory is like a notebook, for storing numbers until they are needed later.)

The keys for putting numbers into the memory and taking them out again are marked differently on different makes of calculator. You will have to find out how yours works. Here we shall use $\boxed{\text{M in}}$ to mean 'put into the memory' and $\boxed{\text{M out}}$ to mean 'take out of the memory'.

To do $\dfrac{779}{18 + 23}$, you do $18 + 23$ first and put the result in the memory. Then divide 779 by the number in the memory.

$\boxed{1}\,\boxed{8}\,\boxed{+}\,\boxed{2}\,\boxed{3}\,\boxed{=}\,\boxed{\text{M in}}\,\boxed{7}\,\boxed{7}\,\boxed{9}\,\boxed{\div}\,\boxed{\text{M out}}\,\boxed{=}$

C2 Do these on your calculator. Check your calculator method by doing the calculations in your head.

(a) $\dfrac{12}{5-2}$ (b) $10 - \dfrac{6}{2}$ (c) $\dfrac{24}{3\times2}$ (d) $\dfrac{9+6}{7-2}$

C3 Do these on your calculator. The answers are all whole numbers.

(a) $\dfrac{2736}{24 \times 19}$ (b) $\dfrac{178 + 446}{13}$ (c) $293 - \dfrac{3525}{141}$

(d) $124 \times (381 - 178)$ (e) $(449 - 362) \times 35$ (f) $847 - (26 \times 33$

C4 Do these on your calculator. Round off each answer to 1 d.p.

(a) $20 \cdot 3 - \dfrac{17 \cdot 6}{2 \cdot 9}$ (b) $\dfrac{48 \cdot 2}{16 \cdot 3 \times 11 \cdot 7}$ (c) $4 \cdot 6 \times (37 \cdot 1 - 19 \cdot 9$

(d) $7 \cdot 65 - (1 \cdot 8 \times 2 \cdot 5)$ (e) $15 \cdot 37 - \dfrac{26 \cdot 2}{0 \cdot 8}$ (f) $\dfrac{15 \cdot 2 + 17 \cdot 9}{0 \cdot 63}$

D Substituting into formulas

Worked example

Use the formula $q = a - bp$ to work out q when a is $50 \cdot 5$, b is $36 \cdot 2$ and p is $0 \cdot 37$. Give the result to 1 d.p.

Start by writing down the formula. $\longrightarrow$ $q = a - bp$

Replace a, b and p by their values.
Write down the calculation you have to do. $\longrightarrow$ $q = 50 \cdot 5 - (36 \cdot 2 \times 0 \cdot 37)$

Notice the **brackets** to show that $36 \cdot 2 \times 0 \cdot 37$ has to be done first.

Now think out how to do it on your calculator. $q = 37 \cdot 1$ (to 1 d.p.)

D1 The formula $T = G - \dfrac{h}{300}$ can be used to find the temperature (roughly) at various heights above the ground.
G stands for the temperature at ground level, in °C.
h stands for the height in metres above the ground.
T stands for the temperature at a height h m above ground level, in °C.

Use the formula to calculate T when

(a) G is 14 and h is 1850   (b) G is 23 and h is 1420

D2 If $a°$ is the size of each angle of a regular polygon with n sides, then a is given by the formula

$$a = 180 - \dfrac{360}{n}$$

Use a calculator to find a when n is   (a) 250   (b) 450   (c) 1500

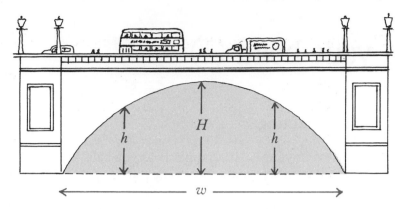

D3 The area of a symmetrical arch shape can be calculated **approximately** from the measurements shown in the diagram.

w is the width of the arch, in metres.
H is the maximum height in m, measured at the middle of the arch.
h is the height measured at either $\frac{1}{4}$ or $\frac{3}{4}$ of the distance across.

The formula which gives the area, A m^2, approximately is

$$A = \frac{w(H + 4h)}{6}.$$

Use this formula to find A when

(a) $H = 13\cdot7$, $h = 9\cdot1$, $w = 43\cdot8$ (b) $H = 8\cdot8$, $h = 5\cdot9$, $w = 23\cdot2$

D4 A factory makes saucepans. The inside surface of each saucepan is coated with a 'non-stick' coating.

Here is the formula for working out the area of the inside surface.

$$S = \pi D\left(\frac{D}{4} + d\right).$$

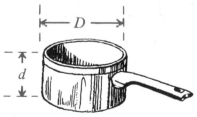

D is the diameter of the saucepan, in cm.
d is the depth of the saucepan, in cm.
S is the inside surface area, in cm^2.
π, as usual, has the value $3\cdot14\ldots$

Calculate S when (a) D is $24\cdot3$ and d is $16\cdot8$ (b) D is $17\cdot9$ and d is $9\cdot4$

D5 When a stone is thrown vertically upwards with a speed of u m/s, its height after t seconds in the air is given by the formula

$$h = ut - 4\cdot9t^2.$$

h is the height in metres.

Calculate h when (a) u is 50 and t is 4 (b) u is $87\cdot5$ and t is $3\cdot5$

Answers to B2:   (a) $24\cdot6$ (b) $42\cdot9$ (c) $22\cdot6$ (d) $21\cdot84$ (e) 6 (f) $6\cdot75$

2 In your head (1)

Adding and subtracting

1 Do these in your head, as quickly as you can. Write the answers.

(a) $8 + 6$ (b) $15 + 7$ (c) $28 + 3$ (d) $7 + 46$ (e) $35 + 9$

(f) $17 - 8$ (g) $24 - 6$ (h) $81 - 5$ (i) $42 - 7$ (j) $63 - 4$

2 Do these in your head, as quickly as you can.

(a) $29 + 30$ (b) $41 + 20$ (c) $63 - 30$ (d) $18 + 40$ (e) $67 - 20$

(f) $22 + 70$ (g) $38 + 60$ (h) $83 - 10$ (i) $27 + 50$ (j) $89 - 50$

You can add a two-figure number in your head by doing it in two steps.

For example to add on 38, you can add 30 first and then 8.

So you can do $45 + 38$ like this.

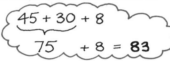

$45 + 30 + 8$

$75 + 8 = \mathbf{83}$

This is not the only way to add on in your head. You may have a way which you find easier. For example, some people would add on 38 by adding 40 first and then subtracting 2.

3 Do these in your head.

(a) $26 + 33$ (b) $47 + 25$ (c) $34 + 57$ (d) $26 + 57$ (e) $18 + 34$

(f) $32 + 46$ (g) $45 + 29$ (h) $67 + 15$ (i) $18 + 36$ (j) $49 + 33$

Here is a problem of the 'how many more?' type.
You are going on a journey of 63 miles. So far you have done 28 miles.
How many more miles are there?

You can do it in your head like this. From 28 to 30 is 2 miles,
from 30 to 63 is 33 miles,
so **35** miles still to go.

This is not the only way to do it. Here are some others.

(1) 28 to 33 is 5   (2) 28 to 58 is 30   (3) 28 to 30 is 2
  33 to 63 is 30   58 to 63 is 5   30 to 60 is 30
    So 35   So 35   32 so far
                    60 to 63 is 3
                      So 35

4   Work out the answer to this question in you head. Explain how
    you did it.

    Tina is saving up for a bike. It costs £85. So far she has saved £46.
    How much more does she need to save?

5   In your head, work out the missing number in each of these.

    (a) 44 + ? = 62   (b) 28 + ? = 61   (c) 14 + ? = 58

    (d) 33 + ? = 82   (e) 58 + ? = 96   (f) ? + 25 = 73

    (g) ? + 17 = 62   (h) ? + 44 = 80   (i) 18 + ? = 72

You can subtract a two-figure number in your head by doing it in
two steps.

For example, to subtract 27 you can subtract 20 first and then 7.

So you can do 53 − 27 like this.

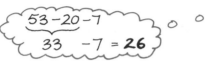

Another way to do it is to think of 53 − 27 as the same as 27 + ? = 53.

Another way is to subtract 30 first and then add on 3.

6   Do these in your head.

    (a) 41 − 25   (b) 86 − 35   (c) 73 − 59   (d) 24 − 17   (e) 53 − 38

    (f) 63 − 47   (g) 95 − 37   (h) 84 − 26   (i) 66 − 29   (j) 83 − 14

7   Do these as quickly as you can in your head.

    (a) A tin of beans costs 27p. How much change do you get from £1?

    (b) My train leaves at 8:46. It is now 8:18. How long have I got?

    (c) I picked 25 lb of apples yesterday and 39 lb today. How much altogether?

    (d) I went shopping with 85p and came back with 36p. How much did I spend?

    (e) It is now 4:43 and the bus goes at 5:18. How long have I got?

    (f) I bought some bananas. I gave the shopkeeper £1 and got 33p change.
         How much did the bananas cost?

    (g) How far is it from Hereford to Worcester?

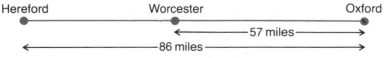

    (h) I went to town by bus and train. The bus fare was 37p and
         the train fare 68p. How much was that altogether?

3 Averages

A The median: a review

The word 'average' has rather a vague meaning when used in everday life.
It means 'not very large, not very small, somewhere about the middle'.
A woman of 'average' height is neither particularly tall nor particularly short.

Here are the heights in cm of 15 women, marked on a scale. The middle woman is
marked with an arrow. (There are 7 women shorter than her and 7 taller.)

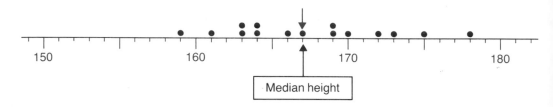

The height of the middle woman is called the **median** height of the group.
The median is often used as an average value.

If there were 16 women in the group, there would be a middle pair instead
of a middle one. In this case the median is taken to be halfway between
the heights of the middle pair.

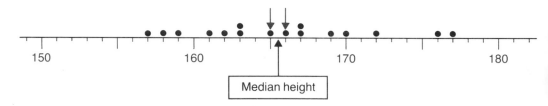

A1 Here are the weekly wages of the 13 employees of a small company.

£108   £132   £144   £116   £172   £155   £153
£114   £95   £120   £125   £188   £160

Arrange these in order of size, smallest first, and write down the
median weekly wage.

A2 These are the marks obtained by 14 pupils in an exam.

65   74   59   43   63   52   48   63   67   85   92   48   90   78

Arrange the marks in order of size. If the same mark occurs twice,
it must be included twice in the list.

Pick out the middle pair of marks, and write down the median mark.

B The mean

Another way of giving an average value of a set of data is to give the **mean**.

The scale below shows the weights of the 8 forwards in a rugby team.

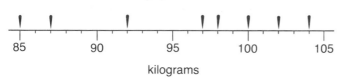

kilograms

The **mean weight** of the 8 forwards is found by adding the weights together and dividing by 8.

$$\text{Mean weight} = \frac{85 + 87 + 92 + 97 + 98 + 100 + 102 + 104}{8} = 95 \cdot 6\,\text{kg}$$
(to 1 d.p.)

Here is the scale again, with the mean marked on it.
Notice that the mean is somewhere 'in the middle' of the weights.
Some of the weights are less than the mean and some are greater.

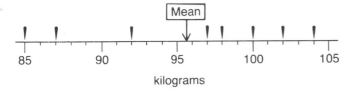

Mean

kilograms

B1 The weights of the 8 forwards in the opposing team are (in kilograms)

84 89 94 97 101 101 104 106

Calculate the mean weight of these forwards, to 1 d.p.

B2 The weights, in kilograms, of the 11 members of a girls' hockey team are

54 63 52 65 55 58 55 59 50 56 47

Calculate the mean weight of the team, to 1 d.p.

B3 Karen kept a record of how many miles she drove each week in her car. Here is the record for the first few weeks of the year.

285 346 316 204 185 223 460 288 229

Calculate Karen's mean weekly mileage during this period, to the nearest mile.

B4 These slow-worms are drawn $\frac{1}{5}$ full-size.
Measure the length of each drawing and write down the
real length of each slow-worm.
Calculate the mean length.

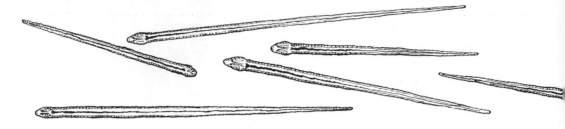

B5 The midday temperature on Monday, Tuesday and Wednesday
was 16°C. On Thursday, Friday, Saturday and Sunday it was
19°C. Calculate the mean midday temperature that week.

Mean values are often used to compare two sets of data.
If the mean weight of a group of boys is 51·6 kg and the mean weight
of a group of girls is 48·7 kg, we say the boys are 'on average'
heavier than the girls.

B6 Jane had seven French tests in a term. Her marks (out of 20)
were 14, 17, 12, 9, 13, 15, 13.
Neeta had eight tests. Her marks
were 11, 10, 7, 13, 16, 16, 18, 14.

(a) Calculate each girl's mean mark, to 1 d.p.

(b) Who did better on average?

B7 These diagrams show two railway lines. In diagram (a) the red
numbers show distances between stations, in miles. In (b) they
show distances from Paddington, in miles.

For each line calculate the mean distance between stations.

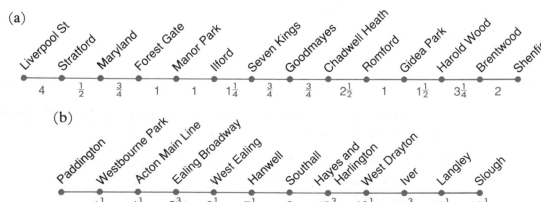

C Calculating the mean from frequencies

Sajda has collected some precious stones. She wants to know the mean weight of the stones.

She weighs each stone and makes a frequency table.

Weight	Frequency (number of stones)
2 g	5
3 g	9
4 g	6
5 g	3
Total	23

Here is the collection itself.

There are 23 stones altogether.

She adds an extra column to the table, to show the weight of each group of stones.

Weight	Frequency (number of stones)	Weight of group
2 g	5	10 g
3 g	9	27 g
4 g	6	24 g
5 g	3	15 g
Total	23	76 g

5 stones, each weighing 2 g, makes 10 g.

9 stones, each weighing 3 g, makes 27 g.

And so on.

This is the total weight of all the stones.

Now she can work out the mean weight of the stones.

The total weight is 76 g. The number of stones is 23.

So the mean weight is $\dfrac{76}{23} = 3 \cdot 3\,\text{g}$, to 1 d.p.

C1 This is the frequency table for another collection of stones.

(a) Copy and complete the table.

(b) Calculate the mean weight of the stones, to 1 d.p.

Weight	Frequency	Weight of group
2 g	7	
3 g	10	
4 g	12	
5 g	4	
Total	33	

11

C2 A firm making matches checked the contents of 100 boxes. The data is in this table.

(a) Copy the table and add a third column showing the number of matches in each group.

(b) Calculate the mean number of matches in a box, to 1 d.p.

Number of matches in box	Frequency (number of boxes
46	8
47	19
48	46
49	15
50	12
Total	100

C3 Philip was making a traffic survey on a road into the centre of a city. He counted the number of people (including the driver) in each car as it passed him. Here is his data.

Calculate the mean number of people in a car, to 1 d.p.

Number of people in car	Number of cars
1	49
2	80
3	35
4	21
5	9
6	2

D Grouped data

This frequency chart shows the weights of all the 12-year-old boys in a school.

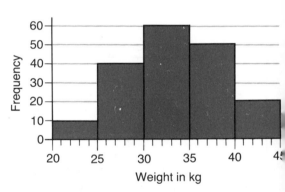

The 'weight' scale is divided into **intervals**: 20–25 kg, 25–30 kg, and so on.

If we want to calculate the mean weight of the boys, we first of all have to find their total weight.
But we cannot do this accurately, because we do not know the weight of each boy. All we know is that there are 10 boys weighing from 20 to 25 kg, and so on.

There is a way of getting a rough value, or **estimate**, of the total weight. We suppose that all the 10 boys in the 20 to 25 kg group have a weight which is halfway between 20 and 25 kg, that is 22·5 kg.

22·5 kg is called the **mid-interval value** of the interval 20 to 25 kg. We do a similar thing for each of the other intervals.

12

D1 (a) What is the mid-interval value of the interval 25 to 30 kg?

(b) Copy and complete the table below. Use the data in the frequency chart on the opposite page.

Weight in kg	Mid-interval value	Number of boys	Weight of group, in kg
20–25	22·5	10	225
25–30			
30–35			
35–40			
40–45			
Total			

10 boys, each 22·5 kg, weigh 225 kg.

Write the total number of boys here.

This total is an **estimate** of the total weight, based on mid-interval values.

(c) Use the estimate of the total weight to calculate an estimate of the mean weight of the boys, to the nearest kg.

D2 This is the frequency chart of the girls' weights in the same school.

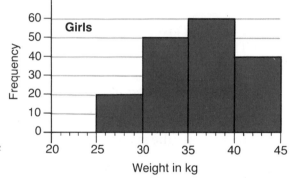

(a) Make a table, like the one in question D1, for the girls' weights.

(b) Calculate an estimate of the mean weight of the girls.

(c) Are the girls heavier or lighter on the whole than the boys?

D3 125 phone calls from a phone box were timed.
This frequency chart was drawn from the data.

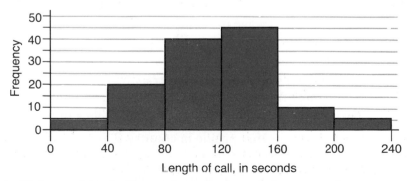

(a) Make a table similar to those in the previous questions.

(b) Calculate an estimate of the mean length of a call.

13

E Averages can mislead

A company employing 11 people says that the mean wage of its employees is £220.

This gives the impression that £220 is a kind of 'middle' figure, with some workers getting a bit more and some a bit less. But how much more, and how much less? The mean tells us nothing about this.

Here are the actual wages of the 11 employees:

 £90   £100   £120   £130   £150   £160   £170   £180   £430   £440   £450

If you add these up and divide by 11, you do get £220 as the mean wage.

Here are the wages marked on a number line, together with the mean wage.

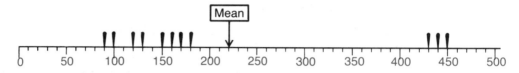

The mean gives a very misleading idea of the employees' wages.
The employees are really split into two separate groups of low and high wage-earners.

It would be more sensible to give the mean of each separate group.

Or we could give the **median** of the whole group, which is £160.
In this case the median gives a fairer idea of the 'average' than the mean.

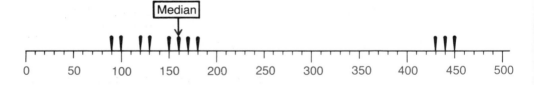

By giving the overall **mean** wage the company may mislead people into thinking that its workers are all quite well-paid.

> **E1** A and B are two different countries.
> In country A people earn, on average, £185 a month.
> In country B people earn, on average, £200 a month.
>
> Does it follow that people in country B are better off than those in country A?
>
> Give reasons for your answer. Discuss them with others in the class.

E2 Here are the ages of the people on a coach outing.

9, 8, 9, 9, 10, 8, 10, 10, 9, 42, 8, 9, 9, 8, 8, 53, 8, 9, 9, 10, 10

(a) Does it make sense to calculate the mean age of the whole group? If not, why not?

(b) Calculate the mean age of the children in the group.

E3 A firm employs 15 people.
Their monthly earnings, in £, are listed on the right in order of size, starting with the least well-paid.

280
280
300
300
310
320
320
330
360
370
650
680
690
850
890

(a) What is the median of the employees' monthly earnings?

(b) The total of all 15 employees' monthly earnings is £6930. (You can check this if you like.)

Calculate the mean of the employees' monthly earnings.

(c) Which value, the median or the mean, gives a better idea of the 'average' monthly earnings in the firm?

(d) Which 'average' – median or mean – would you quote if you were a union leader putting forward a claim for higher pay?

(e) Which would you quote if you were the managing director?

(f) If the mean is used as the average, how many of the 15 workers have 'above average' monthly earnings?

In the example in the previous question, the mean is high because of the high earnings of a few employees. If these few were paid even more, the mean would increase, but the median would stay the same.

E4 20 batteries of a particular make were tested by connecting each one to a bulb and seeing how long the battery lasted. The lifetimes of the batteries, in hours, are given below in order of length, shortest first.

3   4   6   6   7   18   29   33
34   34   35   37   37   37   39   40
40   41   42   42

(a) What is the median of the batteries' lifetimes?

(b) Calculate the mean lifetime of the 20 batteries.

(c) Which value, median or mean, gives a better idea of the 'average' lifetime?

4 Equations and formulas (1)

A Inverse operations and balancing

'Add 3', 'subtract 5', 'multiply by 2', 'divide by 6' are all examples
of **operations**, or things we can do to numbers.

Each of these operations has an **inverse** or 'undoing' operation.

For example, to undo the effect of dividing by 6, we have to multiply by 6.
'Multiply by 6' is the inverse of 'divide by 6'.

We can show this in a diagram; x stands for any starting number.

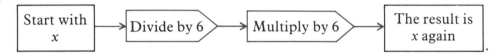

We can write the same thing in symbols:

$\frac{x}{6} \times 6$ is the same as x.

We shall need to use inverse operations in this chapter, which is about
solving equations.

Here are some examples of equations: $\qquad 7x = 91 \qquad 5p - 2 = 38 \qquad \frac{m}{0 \cdot 9} = 1 \cdot 7$

In each equation the letter stands for an unknown number.
Finding the value of the letter is called **solving** the equation.

The method used to solve equations is based on two important ideas:
inverse operations and **balancing**. Balancing means doing the same
thing to both sides of an equation, so that the two sides stay equal.

Worked example

(1) Solve the equation $7x = 91$.

> The left-hand side means the same as $x \times 7$.

> To undo the effect of '$\times 7$' we **divide by 7**.
>
> We do this to **both sides,** to balance the
> equation.

We can check the result fits the equation.

$$7x = 91$$

$$\frac{7x}{7} = \frac{91}{7}$$

$$x = 13$$

Check: When $x = 13$,
$7x = 7 \times 13 = 91$ ✓

In the questions which follow, you may be able to spot the answer straight away. Even so, write out the working as in the worked example. It will be useful practice for later, when answers are difficult to spot.

Check each answer.

A1 Solve these equations.

(a) $5x = 80$ (b) $6x = 132$ (c) $15x = 285$ (d) $37x = 333$

A2 Solve these equations. Give each answer to 1 decimal place.

(a) $7x = 23$ (b) $19x = 230$ (c) $1 \cdot 8x = 5 \cdot 6$ (d) $4 \cdot 5x = 9 \cdot 3$

Worked example

(2) Solve the equation $\dfrac{x}{3} = 15$.

The left-hand side means $x \div 3$.

To undo the effect of '÷3' we **multiply by 3**. We do this to **both sides,** to balance the equation.

$$\frac{x}{3} = 15$$

$$\frac{x}{3} \times 3 = 15 \times 3$$

$$x = 45$$

Check: When $x = 45$

$$\frac{x}{3} = \frac{45}{3} = 15 \checkmark$$

A3 Solve these equations.

(a) $\dfrac{x}{5} = 17$ (b) $\dfrac{x}{14} = 9$ (c) $\dfrac{x}{37} = 18$ (d) $\dfrac{x}{18} = 40$

A4 Solve these equations.

(a) $\dfrac{x}{1 \cdot 5} = 3 \cdot 6$ (b) $\dfrac{x}{2 \cdot 2} = 7 \cdot 5$ (c) $\dfrac{x}{0 \cdot 9} = 0 \cdot 7$

A5 Solve these equations. Give the answer to 1 d.p. where necessary.

(a) $9x = 31$ (b) $\dfrac{x}{8} = 13$ (c) $x - 62 = 17$

(d) $\dfrac{x}{1 \cdot 8} = 55$ (e) $x + 1 \cdot 3 = 2 \cdot 8$ (f) $0 \cdot 6x = 1 \cdot 7$

(g) $x - 2 \cdot 9 = 7 \cdot 6$ (h) $\dfrac{x}{12} = 0 \cdot 7$ (i) $1 \cdot 8x = 4 \cdot 9$

17

B Equations involving two operations (1)

You have solved several equations of this type:

a number $\times x$ = another number

Examples of this type are:

$3x = 6$, $25x = 90$, $1 \cdot 3x = 10 \cdot 4$,   and so on.

This type of equation is called the '$ax = b$' type.

When you have a more complicated equation to solve, you may be able to 'reduce' it to an equation of the $ax = b$ type.

Worked example

(3) Solve the equation $3x + 28 = 70$.

This is not of the $ax = b$ type because of the extra operation $+28$ on the left-hand side. So we first have to undo the '$+28$'.

So we first subtract 28 from both sides.

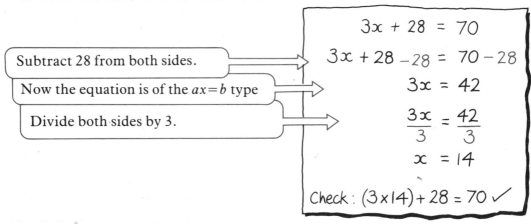

Subtract 28 from both sides.

Now the equation is of the $ax=b$ type

Divide both sides by 3.

$$3x + 28 = 70$$
$$3x + 28 - 28 = 70 - 28$$
$$3x = 42$$
$$\frac{3x}{3} = \frac{42}{3}$$
$$x = 14$$

Check : $(3 \times 14) + 28 = 70$ ✓

B1 Solve these equations.

(a) $2x + 19 = 31$ (b) $4x + 7 = 35$ (c) $5x + 13 = 58$

B2 The equation $4x - 5 = 19$ is not of the $ax = b$ type because of the extra '-5' on the left-hand side.

(a) What do you do to both sides of the equation to undo the '-5'?

(b) Solve the equation.

B3 Solve each of these equations.

(a) $2x - 7 = 9$ (b) $3x - 14 = 7$ (c) $5x - 13 = 22$

(d) $4x + 11 = 39$ (e) $26 = 6x - 10$ (f) $31 = 4 + 3x$

18

B4 Solve these equations. The answers may not be whole numbers, and may be negative.

(a) $2x - 7 = 18$ (b) $3x + 7 = 1$ (c) $15 = 4x - 3$
(d) $3 = 6x - 18$ (e) $8x + 3 = 5$ (f) $8 = 5x + 10$

C Equations involving two operations (2)

In section A you solved several equations of the ' $\dfrac{x}{a} = b$' type.

Examples are: $\dfrac{x}{3} = 15$, $\dfrac{x}{27} = 62$, $\dfrac{x}{0 \cdot 8} = 0 \cdot 6$,   and so on.

Some other types of equation can be 'reduced' to the $\dfrac{x}{a} = b$ type.

Worked example

(4) Solve the equation $\dfrac{x}{5} - 4 = 7$.

Add 4 to both sides.

Now the equation is of the $\dfrac{x}{a} = b$ type

Multiply both sides by 5.

$$\frac{x}{5} - 4 = 7$$

$$\frac{x}{5} - 4 + 4 = 7 + 4$$

$$\frac{x}{5} = 11$$

$$\frac{x}{5} \times 5 = 11 \times 5$$

$$x = 55$$

Check: $\dfrac{55}{5} - 4 = 11 - 4 = 7\checkmark$

C1 Solve these equations.

(a) $\dfrac{x}{4} + 9 = 11$ (b) $\dfrac{x}{6} - 22 = 32$ (c) $\dfrac{x}{7} - 4 = 10$

C2 Solve these equations.

(a) $\dfrac{x}{23} - 17 = 41$ (b) $6 + \dfrac{x}{8} = 13$ (c) $18 + \dfrac{x}{3} = 26$

C3 Solve these equations. Give the answer to 1 d.p. where necessary.

(a) $5x - 7 = 19$ (b) $\dfrac{x}{4} - 25 = 31$ (c) $38 + 7x = 51$

(d) $26 + \dfrac{x}{6} = 50$ (e) $8x + 5 = 17$ (f) $46 = 25 + 2x$

(g) $80 = 5x - 2$ (h) $19 = \dfrac{x}{4} - 3$ (i) $20 = 3 + \dfrac{x}{3}$

D Equations from formulas

Worked example

(5) The formula $I = \dfrac{V}{R}$ is used in electrical calculations.

I stands for the current, in amps.
V stands for the voltage, in volts.
R stands for the resistance, in ohms.

Find the value of V when $I = 18$ and $R = 5$.

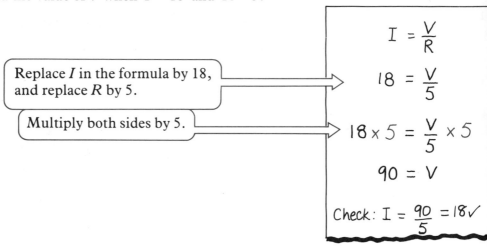

Replace I in the formula by 18, and replace R by 5.

Multiply both sides by 5.

$$I = \frac{V}{R}$$

$$18 = \frac{V}{5}$$

$$18 \times 5 = \frac{V}{5} \times 5$$

$$90 = V$$

Check: $I = \dfrac{90}{5} = 18 \checkmark$

D1 Use the formula $I = \dfrac{V}{R}$ to find

    (a) the value of V when $I = 5$ and $R = 20$

    (b) the value of V when $I = 2{\cdot}6$ and $R = 4{\cdot}5$

D2 The volume of a prism is given by the formula

    $V = Al$.

V is the volume in cm^3.
A is the cross-sectional area in cm^2.
l is the length in cm.

    (a) Find the value of l when $V = 72$ and $A = 4$.

    (b) Find the value of A when $V = 240$ and $l = 32$.

D3 P, F and A are three quantities connected by the formula

    $P = \dfrac{F}{A}$

    (a) Calculate F when $P = 1{\cdot}7$ and $A = 43{\cdot}0$.

    (b) Calculate F when $P = 0{\cdot}42$ and $A = 0{\cdot}6$.

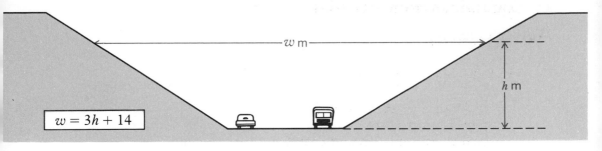

$w = 3h + 14$

D4 The diagram above shows the cross-section of a road cutting.

w metres is the width of the cutting at a height h metres above the level of the road.

w and h are connected by the formula $w = 3h + 14$.

Suppose you want to find the value of h for which w is 50. You replace w in the formula by 50 and get $50 = 3h + 14$.

(a) Solve the equation $50 = 3h + 14$ to find h when w is 50.

(b) Find the value of h for which w is 77.

D5 The formula for this cutting is

$$w = \frac{h}{4} + 12.$$

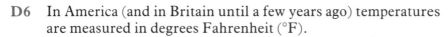

(a) Find the width of the cutting at a height of 10 metres above the bottom.

(b) Find the value of h when w is 17.

(c) Find the value of h when w is 13·5.

(d) How wide is the cutting at the bottom?

D6 In America (and in Britain until a few years ago) temperatures are measured in degrees Fahrenheit (°F).

To convert a temperature from degrees Celsius to degrees Fahrenheit you use the formula

$$f = 1·8c + 32.$$

c is the temperature in °C; f is the temperature in °F.

(a) Calculate f when $c = 15$.

(b) Calculate c when $f = 50$.

(c) Calculate c when $f = 100$, giving the answer to 1 d.p.

E Equations with the unknown on both sides

Worked example

(6) Solve the equation $5x + 11 = 2x + 23$.

      Notice that 'x' appears on both sides of the equation.
We really want 'x' to be on one side only.

      If we subtract $2x$ from both sides, we shall be left with $3x$ on
the left-hand side, and no x at all on the right-hand side.

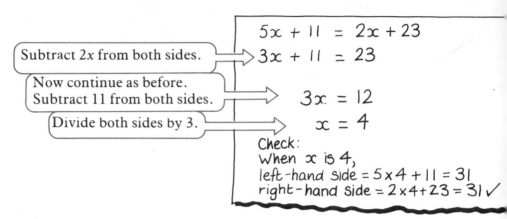

E1 Solve the equation $4x + 5 = 3x + 11$.

E2 Solve the equation $6x + 7 = 4x + 19$.

E3 Solve the equation $3x + 10 = 7x - 2$.

      (Start by subtracting $3x$ from both sides.)

E4 Solve the equation $2x + 15 = 5x$.

E5 Solve the equation $18 + 2x = 3 + 7x$.

E6 Solve the equation $6x - 2 = 22 + 3x$.

The answers to questions E1 to E6 were all positive whole numbers.
The answers to questions E7 to E10 may be negative, and may not
be whole numbers. Check each answer by making sure it fits the equation.

      E7 Solve the equation $7x + 3 = 5x + 12$.

      E8 Solve the equation $2x + 1 = 5x + 7$.

      E9 Solve the equation $8x = 12 + 3x$.

    E10 Solve the equation $9x + 10 = 7x$.

5 Angles

A Review of angle relationships

Angles on one side of a straight line add up to 180°.
(180° means 180 degrees.)

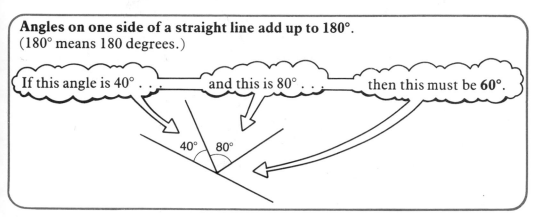

If this angle is 40° . . . and this is 80° . . . then this must be **60°**.

A1 Calculate the angles marked with letters.

(a)
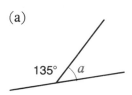
135° a

(b)
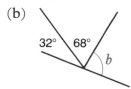
32° 68° b

(c)
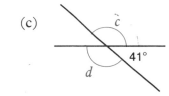
ĉ
41°
d

Angles round a point add up to 360°.

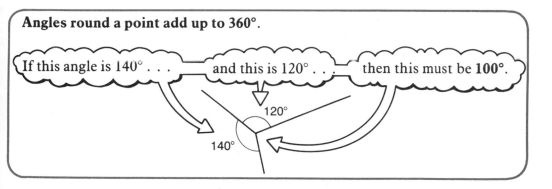

If this angle is 140° . . . and this is 120° . . . then this must be **100°**.

120°
140°

A2 Calculate the angles marked with letters.

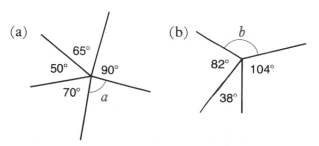

(a)
65°
50° 90°
70° a

(b)
b
82° 104°
38°

23

Straight lines which cross make an **X**.
Opposite angles of an X are equal.

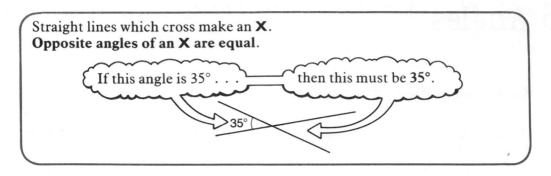

If this angle is 35° . . .   then this must be **35°**.

35°

A3 Calculate the angles marked with letters.

(a)   (b)   (c)

130° *b*   *c*   *d*   75° *f*
a   *h*   *g*
25°   *e*

The angles of a triangle add up to 180°.

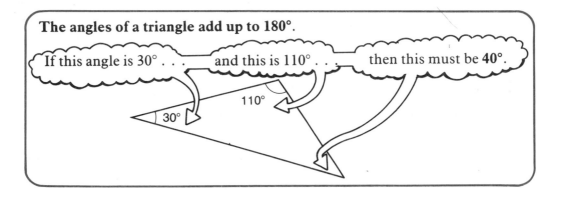

If this angle is 30° . . .   and this is 110° . . .   then this must be **40°**.

30°   110°

A4 Calculate the angles marked with letters.

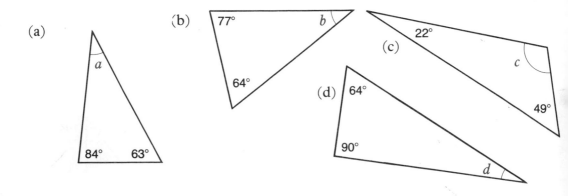

(a)   (b) 77°   *b*   22°   (c)

a   *c*

64°   (d) 64°   49°

84°   63°   90°   *d*

A5 Calculate the lettered angles in these diagrams.

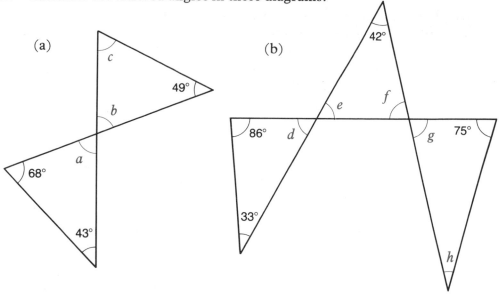

(a)

(b)

A6 Calculate the lettered angles.

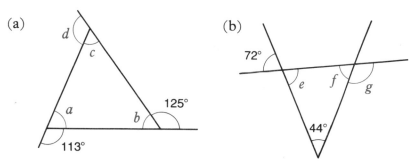

(a)

(b)

A7 Sketch these diagrams.
Fill in the sizes of all the angles.

(a)

(b)

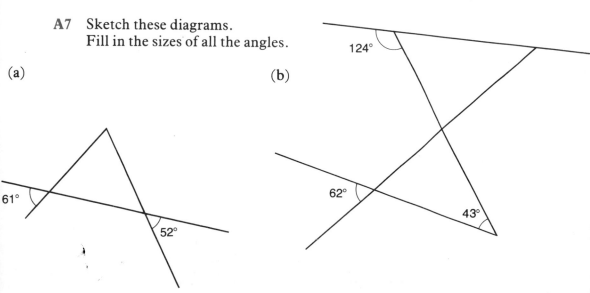

B Angles and parallel lines: 'F-angles'

This is one way to draw a set of parallel lines.
You hold the ruler still and slide the set-square along it.

The marked angles are all copies of the angle of the set-square.

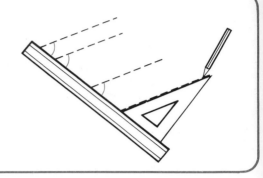

Any pair of parallel lines make an **F**-shape with a line that crosses them.

The marked angles are equal. We shall call them '**F**-angles'.

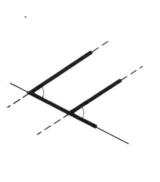

The **F**-shape may be back-to-front or upside down.

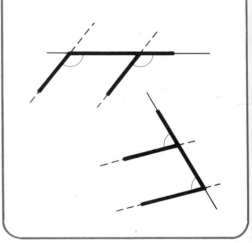

B1   Find the angles marked with letters.

(a)   50°   a

(b)   110°   b

(c)   75°   c   45°   d

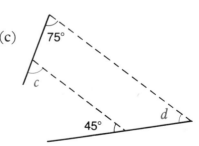

(d)   140°   e   f   115°

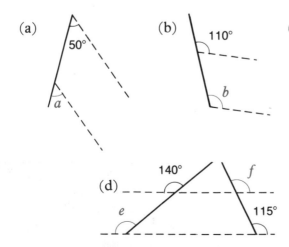

We show parallel lines by arrows, like this.

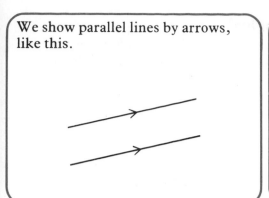

When there are two sets of parallel lines, we use double arrows for the second set, like this.

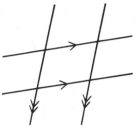

B2 Find the angles marked by letters in the diagrams below.
Look for **F**-shapes. In the first one an **F** is picked out for you.

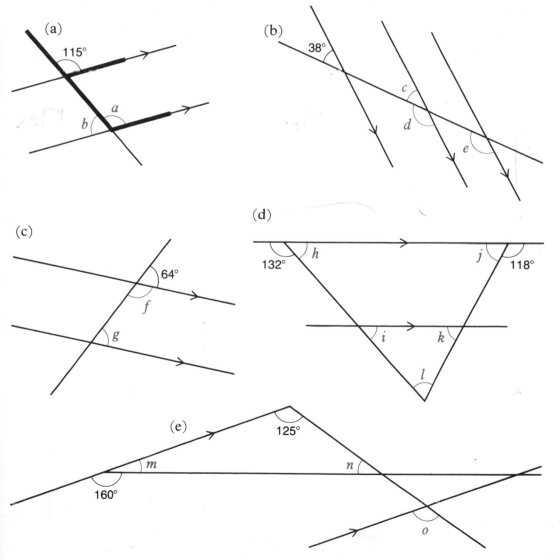

(a)

115°

a

b

(b)

38°

c

d

e

(c)

64°

f

g

(d)

132°   h   j   118°

i   k

l

(e)   125°

m

160°   n

o

C Angles and parallel lines: 'Z-angles'

This **Z** is made by two parallel lines and another line.
One angle is 47°.

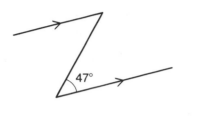

If we extend two of the lines like this, we make an **X** and another angle of 47°.

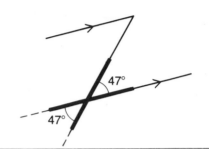

Now we have an **F** as well.
So the top angle must be 47°.

So both angles of the **Z** are 47°.

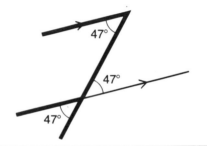

There is nothing special about 47°.
The angles of any **Z** are equal, as long as the top and bottom lines are parallel.

We shall call the angles marked *a* and *b* 'Z-angles'.

Z-angles are equal.

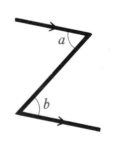

C1 Calculate the lettered angles. Look for **Z**-shapes.
Some have been picked out for you.

(a)

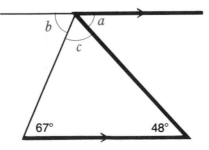

(b)

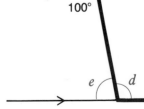

D   Calculating angles

When you are trying to calculate angles in a
diagram, there are a number of things to look for.

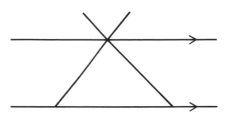

Look for angles on one side
of a line. You know they
add up to 180°.

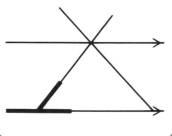

Look for angles round a
point. You know they
add up to 360°.

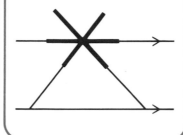

Look for **X**-angles.

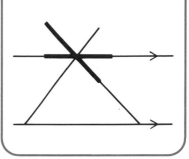

Look for **F**-angles.

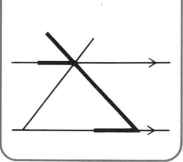

Look for **Z**-angles.

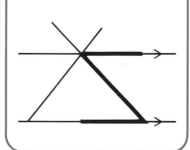

Look for triangles. You
know their angles add up
to 180°.

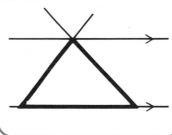

Work out the angles marked with letters in the diagrams below.

D1

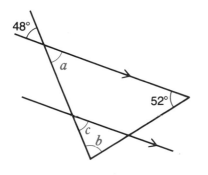

D2

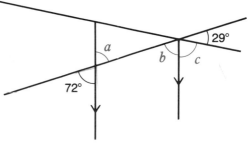

D3

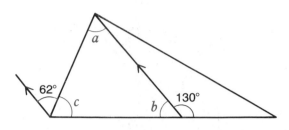

D4

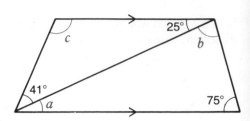

D5 Work out the angles marked
a, *b* and *c*.

It may help if you sketch
the diagram and work out
some of the other angles first.

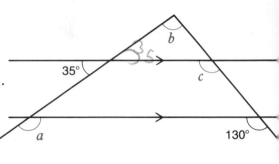

D6 Work out the lettered angles in these diagrams.

(a)

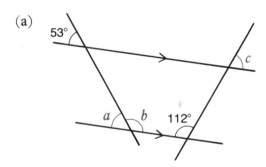

(b)

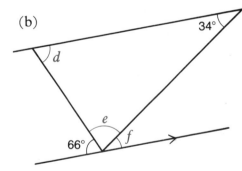

(c)

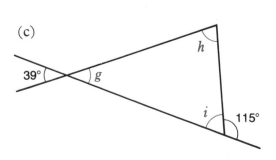

(d)

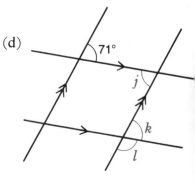

E The angles of a quadrilateral

E1 This quadrilateral is split
into two triangles.

The angles of the triangles are
marked.

(a) Check that the angles of each
triangle add up to 180°.

(b) Write down the sizes of the four
angles at the corners of the
quadrilateral.

(c) Add together the four angles of the quadrilateral.
Can you explain why the result is what it is?

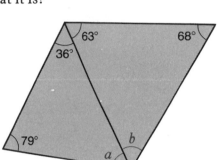

E2 (a) Find the angles *a* and *b*.

(b) Check that the four angles
of the quadrilateral add up to 360°.

There is nothing special about the sizes of the angles in the
previous two quadrilaterals.
Any quadrilateral will split into two triangles, and the sum
of the angles of the quadrilateral will be twice 180°, or **360°**.

E3 Calculate the lettered angles.

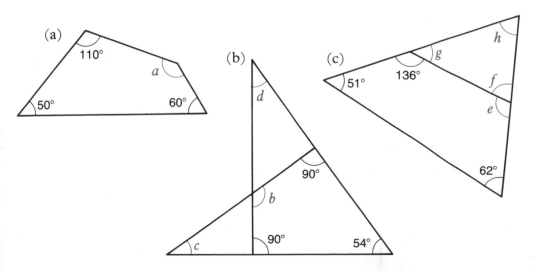

F Isosceles triangles; angle in semicircle

An isosceles triangle has two equal sides and two equal angles.

In diagrams, we show that two lines are of equal length by putting the same mark on them (for example, a dash).

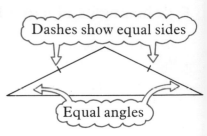

Dashes show equal sides

Equal angles

F1 Calculate the angles marked with letters.

(a)
67°
46b
a67

(b)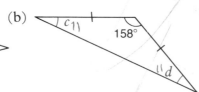
c1)
158°
d

(c)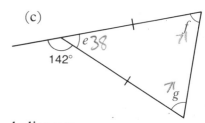
e 38
142°
f
g

F2 Calculate the lettered angles. (Sketch each diagram. You may find it helpful to calculate other angles first.)

(a)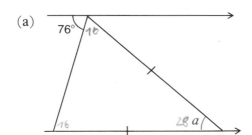
76°
16
28 a

(b)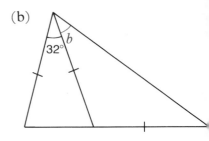
b
32°

The angle in a semicircle

F3 Use compasses to draw a circle, larger than the one shown here.

Draw a diameter of the circle, and label it AB.

The diameter AB divides the circle into two semicircles.

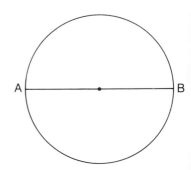

Mark any point P on the circumference of one of the semicircles. Join AP and BP.

Measure the angle APB.

Do it again for other positions of P on the circumference of the semicircle. What do you find?

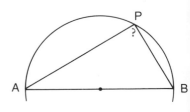

In this diagram of a semicircle, AB is the diameter and C is the centre. P is a point on the semicircle.

Using isosceles triangles we can show the angle APB must always be 90°, no matter where the point P is on the semicircle.

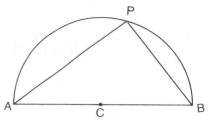

There are no isosceles triangles in the diagram above. But they appear if we draw the line CP.

This is because the three lines CA, CP and CB are all equal to the radius of the circle.

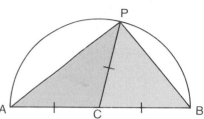

Let *a* stand for the size of the angle at A, and *b* for the size of the angle at B.

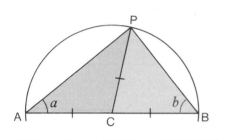

Because the two triangles are isosceles, we can mark another angle of size *a* and another of size *b*.

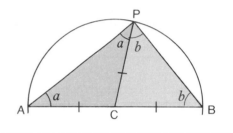

F4 Look at the large triangle APB in the last diagram. The sizes of its three angles are *a*, *a+b* and *b*.

These three angles must add up to 180°, so it follows that
$a + a+b + b = 180°$.

From this explain why the size of angle APB must be 90°.

F5 Calculate the angles marked with letters.

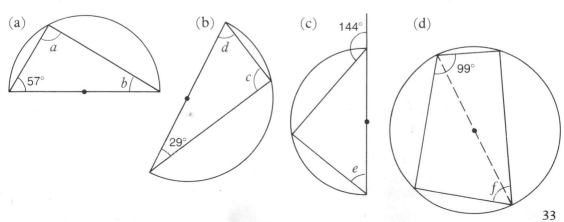

(a)   *a*   57°   *b*

(b)   *d*   *c*   29°

(c)   144°   *e*

(d)   99°   *f*

6 Proportionality (1)

A The multiplier rule

A shop sells curtain material by the metre.
The material costs £4 a metre.

This table shows the costs of different lengths of material.

Length in m	0	1	2	3	4	5	6	7	8	9	10	11	12	13
Cost in £	0	4	8	12	16	20	24	28	32	36	40	44	48	52

If you want 3 metres, you pay £12.
If you **double** the length, the cost is doubled as well.

×2

Length in m	0	1	2	3	4	5	6	7	8	9	10	11	12	13
Cost in £	0	4	8	12	16	20	24	28	32	36	40	44	48	52

×2

If you want 3 times as much, the cost is multiplied by 3.

×3

Length in m	0	1	2	3	4	5	6	7	8	9	10	11	12	13
Cost in £	0	4	8	12	16	20	24	28	32	36	40	44	48	52

×3

If you want 4 times as much, the cost is multiplied by 4, and so on.

When you multiply the length by a number, the cost is multiplied
by the same number.
We say the cost is **proportional** to the length.

A1 The cost of paraffin is proportional to the amount you buy.
5 litres of paraffin costs £2. What is the cost of

(a) 15 litres (3 times as much as 5 litres)

(b) 25 litres   (c) 40 litres   (d) 100 litres

A2 The cost of electric cable is proportional to the length.
3 metres of cable costs £4. What is the cost of

(a) 6 metres (2 times as much as 3 metres)

(b) 12 metres   (c) 30 metres   (d) 60 metres

A3 The weight of a concrete block is proportional to its volume.
$4 \, m^3$ of concrete weighs 9 tonnes. What is the weight of

(a) $12 \, m^3$ (b) $20 \, m^3$ (c) $32 \, m^3$ (d) $40 \, m^3$ (e) $400 \, m^3$

A4 The amount of paint needed to paint a wall is proportional to the area of the wall.

You need 7 litres of paint to cover an area of $30 \, m^2$.
How much paint do you need to cover an area of

(a) $120 \, m^2$ (b) $300 \, m^2$ (c) $3000 \, m^2$ (d) $6000 \, m^2$

A5 The cost of ribbon is proportional to the length you buy.

5cm costs 6p

(a) Calculate the cost of

(i) 20 cm   (ii) 60 cm   (iii) 180 cm   (iv) 1800 cm

(b) How much ribbon can you buy for

(i) 18p   (ii) 180p   (iii) 48p   (iv) £4·80

A6 The cost of a piece of red carpet is proportional to its area.
A piece 3 m by 2 m costs £50.

Calculate the cost of a piece

(a) 8 m by 3 m   (b) 30 m by 2 m

(c) 30 m by 20 m   (d) 3 m by 1 m

B Using a calculator

It is 3 o'clock on a sunny afternoon.
The Lloyd family are waiting for a bus.
Everyone casts a shadow.

Mr Lloyd is 2 times as tall as
his daughter Angela.
So his shadow is 2 times as
long as hers.

The bus stop is 3 times as tall
as Angela. So its shadow is
3 times as long as hers.

In other words, the length of an object's shadow is **proportional** to
the object's height.

Angela's height is 90 cm. Her shadow is 150 cm long.
If we are given the heights of all the other people in the queue, we can
calculate the lengths of their shadows, using the **multiplier rule**.

Mrs Lloyd's height is 165 cm. This is how we can calculate the length of
her shadow.

First calculate the multiplier
from Angela's height to Mrs Lloyd's.

It is $\frac{165}{90} = 1 \cdot 83 \ldots$

Then multiply Angela's shadow
length by the same multiplier.

It is easier to leave $1 \cdot 83 \ldots$ in the
calculator display, and then
multiply by 150.

$1 \cdot 83 \ldots \times 150 \, \text{cm} = \textbf{275 cm}$

B1 Gary Lloyd's height is 171 cm.

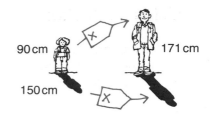

   (a) Calculate the multiplier from Angela's height to Gary's height.

   (b) Calculate the length of Gary's shadow, to the nearest cm.

B2 Sarah Lloyd's height is 120 cm.
Calculate the length of her shadow, to the nearest cm.

B3 A dog comes and sits next to Angela.
Its height is 72 cm.

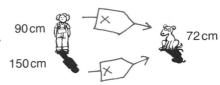

   (a) Calculate the multiplier from Angela's height to the dog's height.

   (b) Calculate the length of the dog's shadow.

B4 The weight of a steel bar of uniform thickness is proportional to the length of the bar.

A bar of length 34 cm weights 860 g.
A second bar is 45 cm long.

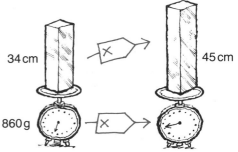

   (a) Calculate the multiplier from the first bar's length to the second.

   (b) Calculate the weight of the second bar.

B5 The volume of water in a container of uniform cross-section is proportional to the depth of the water.

When 8·5 litres of water is poured in, the depth is 35·0 cm.

Calculate the depth when the volume is 5 litres.

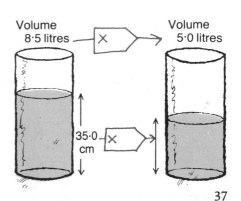

c Scaling up and down

Sam was making a pudding for 10 people. The recipe he was using was for 6 people. It told him to use 500g of sugar to make enough for 6 people.

Sam knew that the amount of sugar had to be proportional to the number of people. So he used the multiplier rule to work out how much sugar he needed.

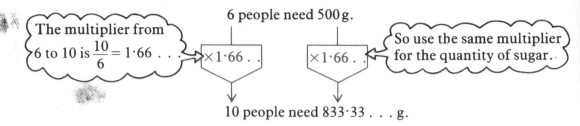

6 people need 500 g.

The multiplier from 6 to 10 is $\frac{10}{6} = 1\cdot66\ldots$

$\times 1\cdot66\ldots$

$\times 1\cdot66\ldots$

So use the same multiplier for the quantity of sugar.

10 people need 833·33 . . . g.

The answer 833·33 . . . g, is much too 'accurate' for cooking!
It is sensible to round it off to the nearest 25 g, and call it 825 g.

C1 A recipe for 6 people requires 400 g of sugar and 1 litre of milk. Calculate the quantities of sugar and milk required for 15 people.

C2 A recipe for 8 people requires 1·5 kg of flour and 10 eggs. Calculate the quantity of flour and the number of eggs required for 30 people.

C3 Sheila made some mortar. She used 12 kg of lime and 28 kg of sand. Now she needs some more mortar. She has 5 kg of lime. How much sand should she mix with it?

C4 Another way to do question C3 is to work out the multiplier from the amount of lime to the amount of sand. Do it this way and check that the answer is the same.

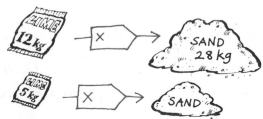

D Non-proportionality

A student weighed some steel ball bearings. Here are her results.

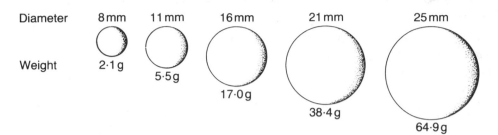

Look at the balls whose diameters are 8 mm and 16 mm.
Their weights are 2·1 g and 17·0 g.

The multiplier from 8 mm to 16 mm is ×2.
But the multiplier from 2·1 g to 17·0 g is **not** ×2.

If weight was proportional to diameter, we would expect the weight of
the 16 mm ball to be twice that of the 8 mm ball, or 4·2 g.
But it isn't. So **weight is not proportional to diameter**.

D1 Look at the 16 mm ball and the 25 mm ball.
Calculate the multiplier from 16 to 25, using a calculator.
Then calculate the multiplier from 17·0 g to 64·9 g.

The two multipliers should be different.

D2 Another student poured different amounts of water into a cone.
Each time she measured the depth of the water and its volume.

Here are her results.

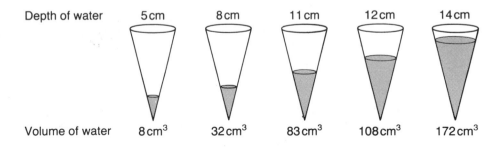

(a) Choose two of the cones. Calculate the multiplier from the depth
in one to the depth in the other. Then calculate the multiplier
from the volume in one to the volume in the other.

(b) Is the volume of water proportional to its depth?

It is easy to see why the volume of water in a cone cannot be proportional to the depth of the water.

Here is some water in a cone.

If you double the depth of the water you do **not** double the volume.

This volume is not equal to this volume.

D3 (a) Copy and complete this table showing the areas of squares.

Length of side, in cm	1	2	3	4	5	6
Area of square, in cm^2						

(b) If you double the length of each side of the square (for example from 3 cm to 6 cm), do you double the area as well?

(c) Is the area of a square proportional to the length of its side?

D4 Make a similar table showing the perimeters of squares instead of areas.

Is the perimeter of a square proportional to the length of its side? Explain how you decide.

D5 (a) Copy and complete this table showing the volumes of cubes.

Length of edge, in cm	1	2	3	4	5	6
Volume of cube, in cm^3						

(b) Is the volume of a cube proportional to the length of its edge? Explain how you decide.

D6 Julie was doing an experiment with a spring.
She hung different weights on the end of the spring, and measured its length each time.

Here are her results.

Weight in kg	2·5	3·5	4·0	5·5	8·5
Length in cm	36	40	42	48	60

Is the length of the spring proportional to the weight on it? Explain how you decided.

7 Equations and formulas (2)

A Equations from formulas

A car travels at a constant speed of s metres per second for t seconds.
If d metres is the distance it travels, then d is given by the formula

$$d = st.$$

This formula tells us how to calculate d when we know s and t.
We say it gives d **in terms of** s and t.
We call d the **subject** of the formula.

We can also use the formula $d = st$ to calculate t when we know d and s.
For example, suppose d is 56 and s is 35.
When we replace d in the formula by 56 and s by 35, we get an
equation to solve.

$$56 = 35t$$

The right-hand side of this equation means $35 \times t$ or $t \times 35$.
To solve the equation we have to divide both sides by 35, so as
to **undo** '$\times 35$'.

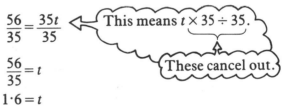

$$\frac{56}{35} = \frac{35t}{35} \quad \longleftarrow \text{This means } t \times 35 \div 35.$$

$$\frac{56}{35} = t \qquad \text{These cancel out.}$$

$$1 \cdot 6 = t$$

A1 a, b and c are connected by the formula $c = ab$.

    (a) Write down the equation you get when c is 85 and a is 34.

    (b) Solve the equation to find b. Write down the steps of the working.

    (c) Write down the equation you get when c is 28 and b is 35.

    (d) Solve the equation to find a.

A2 p, q, r and s are connected by the formula $s = pq + r$.

    (a) Write down the equation you get when s is 23, p is 4 and r is 11.

    (b) Solve the equation to find q. Write out the working.

    (c) Write down the equation you get when s is 17, q is 2 and r is 10.

    (d) Solve the equation to find p.

B Re-arranging a formula

On the previous page we used the formula $d = st$ to calculate t when d and s are known.

If we have to do many calculations of this type, it is better to have a formula for calculating t directly. Then we do not have to solve an equation every time.

So we want a formula for t in terms of d and s.
In other words, we want to make t the **subject** of the formula.

We get the formula for t by thinking of $d = st$ as an equation in which d and s are known numbers, but t is unknown.

We solve the equation in exactly the same way as we would if there were numbers in place of d and s.

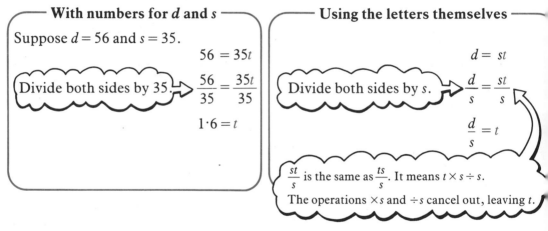

With numbers for d and s

Suppose $d = 56$ and $s = 35$.
$$56 = 35t$$

Divide both sides by 35.
$$\frac{56}{35} = \frac{35t}{35}$$

$$1{\cdot}6 = t$$

Using the letters themselves

$$d = st$$

Divide both sides by s.
$$\frac{d}{s} = \frac{st}{s}$$

$$\frac{d}{s} = t$$

$\frac{st}{s}$ is the same as $\frac{ts}{s}$. It means $t \times s \div s$.
The operations $\times s$ and $\div s$ cancel out, leaving t.

Going from $d = st$ to $\frac{d}{s} = t$ is called **re-arranging** the formula.

B1 (a) Re-arrange the formula $d = st$ to give s in terms of d and t.
Write out the working as in the right-hand panel above.

(b) Use your new formula to find s when d is $6{\cdot}3$ and t is 18.

B2 (a) Re-arrange the formula $f = nw$ to give w in terms of f and n.

(b) Re-arrange the formula $f = nw$ to give n in terms of f and w.

B3 Re-arrange the formula $q = 5p$ to give p in terms of q.

B4 Re-arrange the formula $c = mn$ to give m in terms of c and n.

B5 Re-arrange the formula $c = 3ab$ to give b in terms of c and a.

Worked example

Re-arrange the formula $r = p - a$ to make p the subject.

The right-hand side of the equation is $p - a$.
To get p on its own, we have to undo '$-a$', by adding a.
So we add a to both sides of the equation.

$$r = p - a$$

Add a to both sides. $\Rightarrow$ $r + a = p \underline{- a + a}$

Cancel out

$$r + a = p$$

B6 Re-arrange the formula $y = x + c$ to make x the subject.

B7 Re-arrange the formula $s = r - b$ to make r the subject.

B8 Re-arrange the formula $w = u + v$ to make v the subject.

B9 Re-arrange the formula $y = 7 + x$ to make x the subject.

Worked example

Re-arrange the formula $m = \dfrac{v}{u}$ to make v the subject.

The right-hand side of the equation is $\dfrac{v}{u}$, or $v \div u$.

To get v on its own, we have to undo '$\div u$', by multiplying by u.
So we multiply both sides of the equation by u.

$$m = \frac{v}{u}$$

Multiply both sides by u. $\Rightarrow$ $mu = \dfrac{v}{u} \times u$ $v \div u \times u$

Cancel out

$$mu = v$$

B10 Electricians use the formula $I = \dfrac{V}{R}$.

    (a) Re-arrange the formula so that V is the subject.

    (b) Use your new formula to calculate V when I is $4 \cdot 5$ and R is $0 \cdot 8$.

B11 Make x the subject of each of these formulas.

    (a) $y = a + x$ (b) $y = \dfrac{x}{b}$ (c) $y = x - c$ (d) $y = dx$ (e) $y = x + e$

C Further re-arrangements

So far all the re-arrangements have needed only one step of working, for example multiplying both sides by something.

In this section we will meet re-arrangements which need two steps of working.

If you are not sure what to do, it may help if you replace the letters whose values are supposed to be known, by numbers. Solve the equation you get, and then follow the same steps with the letters themselves.

Example

Re-arrange $v = u + at$ to give a in terms of v, u and t.

We suppose v, u and t are known, and we want to find a.

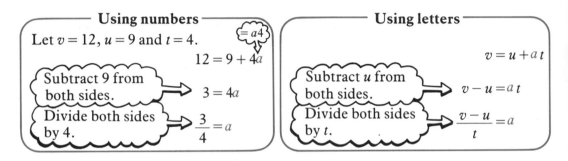

After some practice, you should be able to work with the letters directly.

It is important to do things in the right order.
If you divide both sides by t first, you get this:

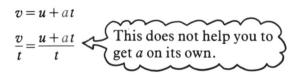

$$v = u + at$$

$$\frac{v}{t} = \frac{u + at}{t}$$

This does not help you to get a on its own.

C1 Re-arrange the formula $y = ax + b$ to give x in terms of y, a and b.
(Subtract b from both sides first.)

C2 Re-arrange the formula $s = cr - d$ to give r in terms of s, c and d.
(Add d to both sides first.)

C3 Re-arrange each of these formulas to make the letter printed in red the subject of the formula.

(a) $q = 4p + a$ (b) $q = kp + a$ (c) $q = kp + a$

(d) $q = k + ap$ (e) $m = af - t$ (f) $w = u + kv$

(g) $w = ku - v$ (h) $w = u + kv$ (i) $t = mp - n$

Worked example

Re-arrange $c = \dfrac{a}{n} + b$ to give a in terms of c, n and b.

Think of the formula as an equation, with a as the letter whose value you want.

$\quad\quad c \quad\quad = \dfrac{a}{n} + b$

Subtract b from both sides.

$\quad\quad c - b \quad = \dfrac{a}{n}$

Now multiply both sides by n.
Notice the **brackets**. They show that the **whole** of the left-hand side is multiplied by n.

$\quad\quad n(c - b) = a$

C4 Re-arrange the formula $k = \dfrac{s}{p} - a$ to give s in terms of k, a and p.

C5 Re-arrange the formula $d = a + \dfrac{c}{n}$ to give c in terms of d, a and n.

C6 Re-arrange each of these formulas to make x the subject.

(a) $q = \dfrac{x}{p} - r$ (b) $r = q + \dfrac{x}{p}$ (c) $p = \dfrac{x}{r} + q$

D Mixed examples

D1 Re-arrange the formula $m = \dfrac{v}{u}$ to make v the subject.

D2 Re-arrange the formula $l = aw + b$

(a) to make w the subject   (b) to make a the subject

D3 Re-arrange the formula $w = cx - d$

(a) to make x the subject   (b) to make c the subject

D4 Re-arrange the formula $s = \dfrac{t}{3} + f$ to make t the subject.

D5 Re-arrange the formula $y = \dfrac{x}{4} - a$ to make x the subject.

D6 Re-arrange the formula $w = 3u - x$ to make x the subject.

D7 Re-arrange the formula $q = \dfrac{x}{t} - s$ to make x the subject.

8 Gradient

A Steepness

'20%' on the road sign tells you the steepness of the hill.
Here is a side view, or **profile**, of the hill.

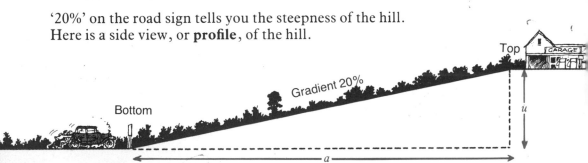

The **horizontal distance** from the bottom of the hill to the top
is marked a (for 'across').
The **change in height** is marked u (for 'up').

'The steepness is 20%' means that u is 20% of a.

A1 What would u be if a were

(a) 100 m   (b) 300 m   (c) 40 m   (d) 60 m   (e) 90 m

A2 The steepness of this hill is 12%.

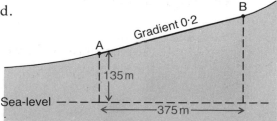

Work out u when a is

(a) 100 m   (b) 300 m   (c) 40 m   (d) 60 m   (e) 90 m

(f) Is this hill steeper than the previous one?

Another word for 'steepness' is **gradient**.
In mathematics we usually write gradients as decimals, not percentages.

The decimal equivalent of 20% is 0·20, or 0·2. So the gradient of
a 20% hill is 0·2.

A3 What is the gradient, as a decimal, of
(a) a 15% hill   (b) a 17% hill   (c) a 7% hill   (d) a 30% hill

A4 This hill's gradient is 0·4. So u is 0·4 of a.
To find u, you multiply a by 0·4.

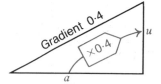

What is u when a is
(a) 70 m   (b) 96 m   (c) 200 m

A5 Calculate u in each of these.

(a)

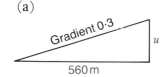

560 m

(b)

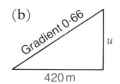

420 m

(c)

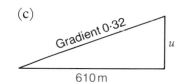

610 m

A6 PQ is part of a cliff path.
The gradient of PQ is 0·3.

P is 56 m above sea-level.
The horizontal distance between
P and Q is 103 m.

u is the change in height as you
go from P to Q.

(a) Calculate u.

(b) Calculate the height of Q
above sea-level.

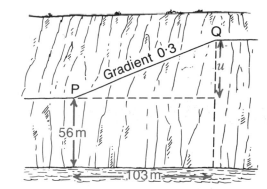

A7 This diagram shows part of a road.

Calculate the height of B above
sea-level.

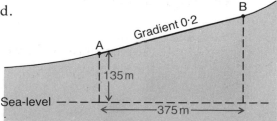

Up to now all gradients have been less than 1.
But a gradient can be greater than 1.

The gradient of this ladder is 2·5.

The distance up is 2·5 times the distance across.

A8 The gradient of a ladder is 1·6. The bottom is 4·5 m from a wall. How far up the wall does the ladder reach?

A9 The bottom of a ladder is 3·7 m from a wall.
The gradient of the ladder is 1.
(a) How far up the wall does the ladder reach?
(b) What angle does the ladder make with the ground?

B Calculating gradients

Look again at the diagram of the ladder at the top of the page.

If you did not know the gradient you could calculate it from the distance across and the distance up.

The gradient is the multiplier from 2 m to 5 m.

So it is the ratio $\frac{5}{2}$, which is 2·5.

$$\text{Gradient} = \frac{\text{Change in height}}{\text{Horizontal distance}}$$

B1 Calculate the gradient of this hill, as a decimal.

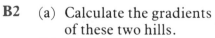

420 m

63

B2 (a) Calculate the gradients of these two hills.
(b) Which hill is steeper?

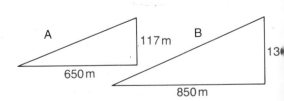

A   117 m   B

650 m   130

850 m

B3 Calculate the gradient of a ladder when the bottom is 1·8 m from a wall and the top is 6·3 m up the wall.

B4 This is a scale drawing of a hill.
The scale is 1 cm to 10 m.

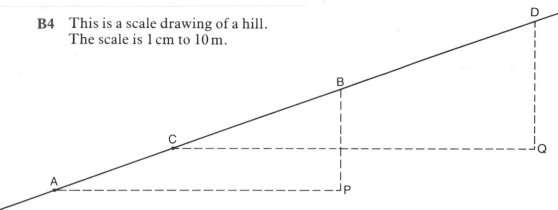

(a) Measure the horizontal distance from A to B. (It is AP.)
Measure the change in height from A to B. (It is PB).
Calculate the gradient of the hill from these two measurements.

It is the ratio $\dfrac{PB}{AP}$. Give the result to 2 decimal places.

(b) Measure the horizontal distance from C to D, and the
change in height from C to D.
Calculate the gradient of the hill from these two measurements.

(c) Measure the horizontal distance and change in height
from C to B. Use them to calculate the gradient of the hill.

You should get the same value for the gradient in all three parts of
question B4. If they are slightly different, it is because measurements
cannot be exact.

You get a more accurate result the larger the triangle you measure.
This . . .   is better than this . . .

but if you could measure **exactly**, both would give the same gradient.

B5 This is a scale drawing of a hill.
Pick two points on the hill, a long
way apart. Find the horizontal
distance and the change in height
between them.
Calculate the gradient
of the hill, to 2 d.p.

49

Railway gradients

If a hill on a railway line is too steep, the engine's wheels
will slip on the rails. The steepest gradient an ordinary
engine can cope with is 0·09.

Mountain railways sometimes use the 'rack and pinion' system.
A toothed wheel (the pinion) on the engine runs along a
toothed rail (the rack).

By this method the gradient can go up to 0·125.
If there is only a single car, the gradient can be up to 0·5.

In a funicular railway, the car is fixed to a cable
which pulls it up the hill.
The steepest funicular railway has a gradient of 0·89.

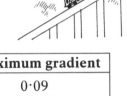

This information is summarised in the table below.

Method of working	Maximum gradient
Ordinary	0·09
Rack and pinion (train)	0·125
Rack and pinion (single car)	0·5
Funicular	0·89

B6 Find the gradient of each of these railways, to 2 decimal places.
Write down a method of working which would be suitable for each one.

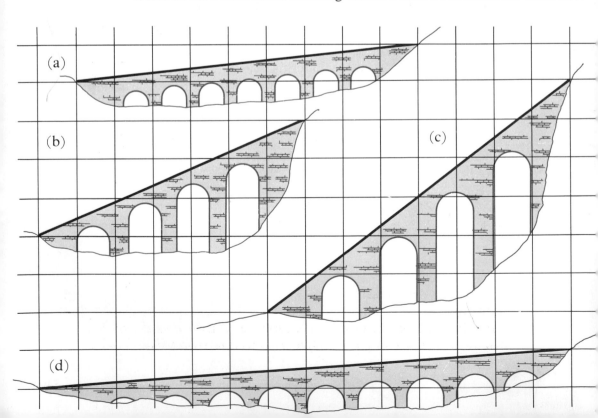

Review 1

1 Using a calculator

1.1 Do these on your calculator. Round off the answer to 2 d.p., where necessary.

(a) $6 \cdot 3 \times (30 \cdot 3 - 18 \cdot 7)$ (b) $\dfrac{49 \cdot 7}{26 \cdot 8 \times 4 \cdot 2}$ (c) $8 \cdot 5 - \dfrac{4 \cdot 9}{1 \cdot 7}$

1.2 In a women's magazine it says that you can find out if you are overweight by dividing your weight in kilograms by the square of your height in metres. If the result is more than 25, then you may be overweight.

Janice is $1 \cdot 68$ m tall and weighs $67 \cdot 2$ kg. Is she overweight?

1.3 If $r = a(p - q)$, calculate r when $a = 0 \cdot 86$, $p = 4 \cdot 09$ and $q = 1 \cdot 76$.

3 Averages

3.1 The weights of the girls in a netball team are, in kg,

$48 \cdot 3, 51 \cdot 7, 56 \cdot 7, 53 \cdot 8, 54 \cdot 4, 50 \cdot 2, 49 \cdot 8$.

The weights of the girls in a hockey team are, in kg,

$49 \cdot 6, 53 \cdot 2, 47 \cdot 7, 56 \cdot 7, 51 \cdot 0, 55 \cdot 3, 45 \cdot 4, 58 \cdot 2, 57 \cdot 8, 46 \cdot 2, 43 \cdot 7$.

(a) Calculate the mean weight of the girls in the netball team, to the nearest $0 \cdot 1$ kg.
(b) Do the same for the girls in the hockey team.
(c) Which team is heavier on average?

3.2 Sally was studying peas for a biology project. She picked some pea-pods from one plant, and counted the peas in each pod. Her data is in the table below.

Number of peas in pod	Frequency (number of pods)
4	8
5	11
6	16
7	10

Copy the table and add a third column showing the number of peas in each group of pods. Calculate the mean number of peas in a pod, to 1 d.p.

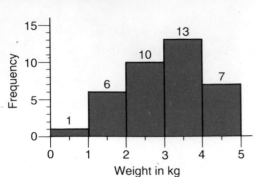

3.3 This is the frequency chart of the weights of the babies born in a hospital during one month.

The weights have been grouped in interval 0–1 kg, 1–2 kg, etc.

(a) What is the mid-interval value for the interval 0–1 kg?

(b) Copy and complete the table below and estimate the mean weight of the babies.

Weight in kg	Mid-interval value	Frequency	Weight of group, in kg
0–1		1	
1–2		6	

4 Equations and formulas (1)

4.1 Solve these equations.

(a) $4x + 29 = 61$ (b) $26 = 3x - 25$ (c) $\frac{x}{5} - 13 = 52$

4.2 u, a and t are connected by the formula $v = u + at$.

(a) Calculate u, given that $v = 46\cdot3$, $a = 4\cdot2$, $t = 25$.

(b) Calculate a, given that $v = 60\cdot7$, $u = 21\cdot5$, $t = 30$.

4.3 Solve these equations.

(a) $5x + 17 = 9x + 5$ (b) $32 + x = 6x + 17$

(c) $0\cdot9x - 1\cdot6 = 5\cdot6$ (d) $\frac{x}{1\cdot63} = 0\cdot8$ (e) $2\cdot8 = 1\cdot9 + \frac{x}{0\cdot4}$

5 Angles

5.1 Calculate the angles marked with letters in these diagrams.

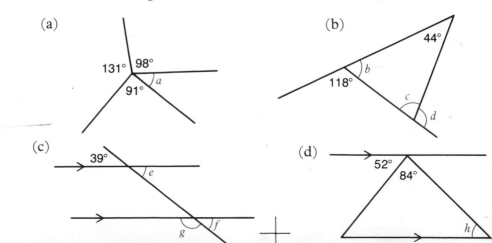

(a)

(b)

(c)

(d)

5.2 Calculate the angles marked with letters in these diagrams.

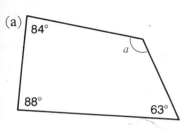

(a) 84° a 88° 63°

(b) 37° b 41° 78°

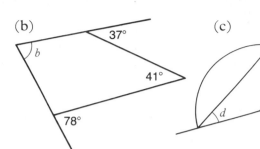

(c) c d 54°

6 Proportionality (1)

6.1 A garden centre sells fertiliser. The cost is proportional to the amount bought. 4 kg of fertiliser costs £7·50.

What is the cost of

(a) 20 kg (b) 32 kg (c) 320 kg (d) 400 kg (e) 4 tonnes

6.2 The electrical resistance of wire is measured in ohms. The resistance of a piece of copper wire of a certain diameter is proportional to the length of the wire.

A piece of length 7·5 m has a resistance of 4·2 ohms.

Calculate the resistance of a piece of length 4·0 m.

6.3 Karl planted grass seed and made a rectangular lawn 20 m by 15 m. He used 80 kg of grass seed.
Fiona wants to plant a lawn 40 m by 12 m. How much grass seed does she need?

6.4 Photographic enlargements are made from negatives, which are of various different sizes. A popular size is 3·6 cm by 2·4 cm.
If one of these negatives is enlarged to make a print whose longer sides are 25 cm long, what will be the length of the shorter sides, to the nearest 0·1 cm?

7 Equations and formulas (2)

7.1 Make V the subject of the formula $R = \dfrac{V}{T}$.

7.2 p, q and r are connected by the formula $p = 2q + r$.

Make (a) r (b) q the subject of the formula.

7.3 Re-arrange each of these formulas to make the letter printed in red the subject of the formula.

(a) $p = q - s$ (b) $p = aq - s$ (c) $p = aq - s$

(d) $y = ax + b$ (e) $y = ax + b$ (f) $y = ax - b$

(g) $z = \dfrac{l}{d}$ (h) $m = \dfrac{a}{f} + b$ (i) $y = \dfrac{x}{k} - a$

8 Gradient

8.1 The gradient of this hill is $0\cdot45$.
Calculate u when a is

(a) 200 m   (b) 60 m   (c) 55 m   (d) 180 m

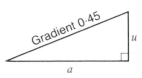

8.2 Calculate the gradients of these hills, to 2 decimal places.

(a)

(b)

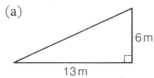
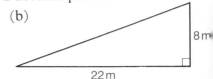

8.3 Find the gradient of this hill, to 2 decimal places.

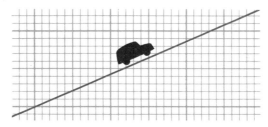

8.4 The bottom end of a ladder is $2\cdot3$ m from a wall.
The gradient of the ladder is $3\cdot5$.
How far up the wall does the ladder reach?

M Miscellaneous

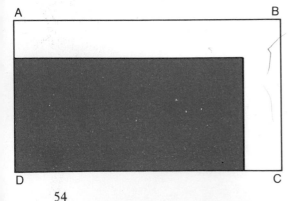

(a) Estimate what percentage of the area of rectangle ABCD is coloured. Write down your estimate.

(b) Measure the sides of ABCD and the sides of the coloured rectangle. Calculate the area of each rectangle.

(c) Calculate the percentage of the area of ABCD which is coloured.

9 In your head (2)

Multiplication and division

1 Write down the answers to these as quickly as you can.

(a) 4×3 (b) 5×4 (c) 6×3 (d) 3×9 (e) 8×5 (f) 7×7

(g) 4×8 (h) 6×6 (i) 5×7 (j) 9×4 (k) 5×5 (l) 7×4

2 Write down the answers to these as quickly as you can.

(a) 3×8 (b) 5×6 (c) 2×7 (d) 8×8 (e) 3×7 (f) 2×9

(g) 4×4 (h) 9×5 (i) 6×4 (j) 3×5 (k) 6×7 (l) 9×8

3 Write down the answers to these as quickly as you can.

(a) $20 \div 2$ (b) $40 \div 5$ (c) $16 \div 8$ (d) $18 \div 3$ (e) $24 \div 4$ (f) $30 \div 5$

$\frac{24}{3}$ ('24 over 3') means the same as $24 \div 3$.

4 Write down the answers to these as quickly as you can.

(a) $\frac{24}{3}$ (b) $\frac{15}{5}$ (c) $\frac{20}{4}$ (d) $\frac{27}{3}$ (e) $\frac{36}{9}$ (f) $\frac{50}{5}$ (g) $\frac{28}{4}$

(h) $\frac{16}{2}$ (i) $\frac{32}{8}$ (j) $\frac{45}{9}$ (k) $\frac{36}{6}$ (l) $\frac{24}{6}$ (m) $\frac{20}{10}$ (n) $\frac{64}{8}$

5 Do these as quickly as you can.

(a) 30×4 (b) 2×40 (c) 5×30 (d) 6×40 (e) 7×30 (f) 8×40

(g) 9×20 (h) 30×6 (i) 40×5 (j) 60×5 (k) 80×3 (l) 7×40

You can do 4×23 in your head like this:

Think of twenty-three as **twenty** and **three**. | 4 twenties are 80. 4 threes are 12. | 80 + 12 = **92**

6 Do these in your head.

(a) 5×13 (5 **tens** and 5 **threes**) (b) 3×24 (c) 4×21

(d) 7×14 (e) 5×18 (f) 5×28 (g) 6×14 (h) 3×17

(i) 16×6 (same as 6×16) (j) 12×8 (k) 14×7 (l) 16×4

10 Equations and formulas (3)

A The density formula

The diagram below shows three metals, and how much $1\,\text{cm}^3$ of each one weighs.

Gold
$1\,\text{cm}^3$ weighs $19\cdot3\,\text{g}$.

Copper
$1\,\text{cm}^3$ weighs $8\cdot9\,\text{g}$.

Aluminium
$1\,\text{cm}^3$ weighs $2\cdot7\,\text{g}$.

$1\,\text{cm}^3$ of gold weighs $19\cdot3\,\text{g}$.
We say the **density** of gold is **$19\cdot3\,\text{g per cm}^3$.**

A1 This diagram shows a block made of
pure nickel.
The block weighs $106\cdot8\,\text{g}$.

(a) How many cubic centimetres of
nickel are there in the block?

(b) How much does $1\,\text{cm}^3$ weigh?

(c) Write down the density of nickel.

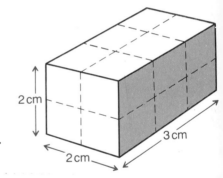

To find the density of nickel you divided the **mass** ($106\cdot8\,\text{g}$) by the
volume ($12\,\text{cm}^3$).

The formula for calculating the density is $D = \dfrac{M}{V}$.

D is the density in g per cm^3; M is the mass in g; V is the volume in cm^3.

A2 A piece of steel whose volume is $3\cdot5\,\text{cm}^3$ has a mass of $27\cdot5\,\text{g}$.
Calculate the density of steel, to the nearest $0\cdot1\,\text{g per cm}^3$.

A3 Calculate the densities of iron, lead and zinc from the following
information. Round off each answer to the nearest $0\cdot1\,\text{g per cm}^3$

(a) A piece of iron whose volume is $33\cdot8\,\text{cm}^3$ weighs $266\cdot0\,\text{g}$.
(b) A piece of lead whose volume is $25\cdot9\,\text{cm}^3$ weighs $292\cdot7\,\text{g}$.
(c) A piece of zinc whose volume is $49\cdot3\,\text{cm}^3$ weighs $352\cdot0\,\text{g}$.

B Using $D = \dfrac{M}{V}$ to calculate M or V

So far we have used the density formula $D = \dfrac{M}{V}$ to calculate D when we know M and V.

The formula can also be used to calculate M when D and V are known or to calculate V when D and M are known.

Here first are some questions in which M is wanted.

B1 Use the formula $D = \dfrac{M}{V}$ to calculate M when D is 7 and V is 4.

(Replace D and V in the formula by their known values, and get an equation for M. Solve the equation.)

B2 Use the formula $D = \dfrac{M}{V}$ to calculate M when D is 8·5 and V is 14.

Calculating V: worked example

Use the formula $D = \dfrac{M}{V}$ to calculate V when D is 3 and M is 15.

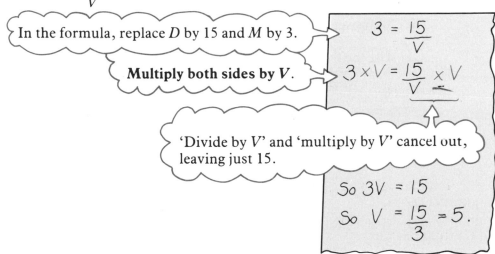

In the formula, replace D by 15 and M by 3.

Multiply both sides by V.

'Divide by V' and 'multiply by V' cancel out, leaving just 15.

$$3 = \frac{15}{V}$$

$$3 \times V = \frac{15}{V} \times V$$

$$\text{So } 3V = 15$$

$$\text{So } V = \frac{15}{3} = 5.$$

This is the first time we have multiplied both sides of an equation by a letter instead of a number.

We can check that the answer is correct by going back to the formula and re-calculating D.

$$D = \frac{M}{V} = \frac{15}{5} = 3 \checkmark$$

B3 Use the formula $D = \dfrac{M}{V}$ to calculate V when D is 8 and M is 12.

Set out the working as shown above. Check the answer.

B4 Solve the equation $18 = \dfrac{270}{x}$ by first multiplying both sides by x.

B5 Solve these equations.

(a) $48 = \dfrac{576}{x}$ (b) $15 = \dfrac{25 \cdot 5}{y}$ (c) $0 \cdot 99 = \dfrac{6 \cdot 93}{p}$

B6 a, b and c are connected by the formula $c = \dfrac{a}{b}$.

Calculate b when c is 4 and a is 30. Check the answer.

B7 Use the formula $I = \dfrac{V}{R}$ to calculate R when $I = 0 \cdot 5$ and $V = 6 \cdot 0$.

B8 Use the formula $P = \dfrac{F}{A}$ to calculate A when $F = 4 \cdot 2$ and $P = 163$.

Give the answer to 2 significant figures.

B9 Use the formula $V = \dfrac{W}{I}$ to calculate I when $V = 240$ and $W = 150$.

C Miscellaneous calculations from formulas

Give all answers correct to 2 significant figures.

C1 Use the formula $F = ma$ to calculate

(a) a when F is $7 \cdot 5$ and m is $4 \cdot 6$
(b) m when F is 280 and a is 48

C2 Use the formula $A = \dfrac{G}{d}$ to calculate

(a) G when A is 8 and d is 4
(b) d when G is 32 and A is $5 \cdot 6$

C3 Use the formula $s = ut$ to calculate

(a) u when $s = 31 \cdot 5$ and $t = 0 \cdot 6$
(b) t when $s = 425$ and $u = 85$

C4 Builders sometimes use the formula $S = \dfrac{M}{L}$.

M stands for the maximum load a beam will carry without breaking.
L stands for the load the beam will actually carry.
S stands for the 'safety factor'.

(a) Calculate S if L is 3500 and M is 16 800.

(b) Calculate M if L is 750 and S is $5 \cdot 5$.

(c) Calculate L if S is $7 \cdot 5$ and M is 42 500.

D Re-arranging formulas

The formula $D = \dfrac{M}{V}$ can be re-arranged either to make M the subject or to make V the subject.

Making M the subject (M in red)	Making V the subject (V in red)
$D = \dfrac{M}{V}$	$D = \dfrac{M}{V}$
Multiply both sides by V. $DV = M$	Multiply both sides by V. $DV = M$
	Divide both side by D. $V = \dfrac{M}{D}$

D1 Re-arrange the formula $I = \dfrac{V}{R}$ to make V the subject.

D2 Re-arrange the formula $I = \dfrac{V}{R}$ to make R the subject.

Worked examples

(1) Re-arrange $s = \dfrac{au}{bc}$ to give u.

$$s = \frac{au}{bc}$$

Multiply both sides by bc. → $sbc = au$

Divide both sides by a. → $\dfrac{sbc}{a} = u$

(2) Re-arrange $r = \dfrac{s}{kt}$ to give t.

$$r = \frac{s}{kt}$$

Multiply both sides by kt. → $rkt = s$

Divide both sides by rk. → $t = \dfrac{s}{rk}$

D3 Re-arrange each of these formulas to give the letter in red.

(a) $l = \dfrac{m}{nz}$ (b) $l = \dfrac{m}{nz}$ (c) $a = \dfrac{be}{cx}$

(d) $a = \dfrac{be}{cx}$ (e) $F = \dfrac{PT}{R}$ (f) $f = \dfrac{A}{5n}$

(g) $Y = \dfrac{Fl}{Ae}$ (h) $Y = \dfrac{Fl}{Ae}$ (i) $v = \dfrac{2at}{sx}$

11 Area

A The area of a parallelogram

A **parallelogram** is a quadrilateral (4-sided shape) in which both pairs of opposite sides are parallel.

P is a parallelogram.
It stands on a 'base' of length b.
Its height, measured at right-angles to the base, is h.

Enclose the parallelogram in a rectangle, like this.
The rectangle is made up of two right-angled triangles A and B, and the parallelogram P.

Area of red rectangle = P + A + B.

Slide triangle A to the right, like this.
Now the same red rectangle is made up of A, B and the rectangle R. So

Area of red rectangle = R + A + B.

So P must have the same area as R.
So the area of P is equal to **bh**.

Any side of a parallelogram can be chosen as the 'base'.
But the 'height' must be measured at right-angles to the base.

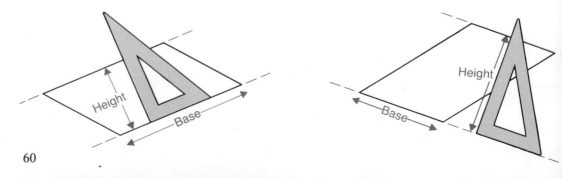

60

You need worksheet R2–1.
The diagrams for questions A1 and A2 are on the worksheet.

A1 There are two copies of this diagram on the worksheet, one for part (a) and one for part (b).

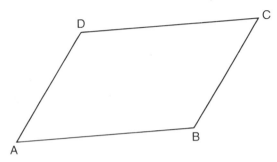

(a) Think of AB as the base of the parallelogram.
Measure the base AB.
Draw the height at right-angles to the base, and measure it.
Calculate the area, to the nearest $0 \cdot 1 \, \text{cm}^2$.

(b) Now think of BC as the base.
Measure the base BC, and the height at right-angles to BC.
Calculate the area, to the nearest $0 \cdot 1 \, \text{cm}^2$.

A2 Find the area of each parallelogram on the worksheet.
Write down which side you use as the base.
Round off each area to the nearest $0 \cdot 1 \, \text{cm}^2$.

A3 (a) Calculate the area, in square units, of the parallelogram PQRS.

(b) Calculate the area of the parallelogram with corners at $(^-3, \, ^-3), (2, 4), (4, 4)$ and $(^-1, \, ^-3)$.

(c) Calculate the area of the parallelogram with corners at $(^-2, 4), (^-2, \, ^-2), (3, \, ^-3)$ and $(3, 3)$.

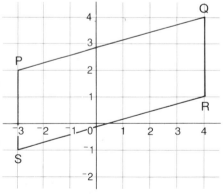

A4 Find the area of the printed part of this stamp, in cm^2 (to the nearest $0 \cdot 1 \, \text{cm}^2$).

B The area of a triangle

A triangle of base b and height h . . .

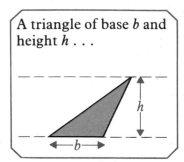

. . . is **half** of a parallelogram. So its area is $\frac{1}{2}bh$.

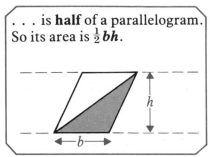

Once again, h must be at right-angles to b.

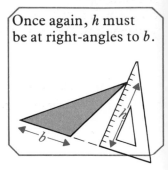

The diagrams for questions B1 and B2 are on worksheet R2–2.

B1 There are three copies of this diagram on worksheet R2–2, one for each part of the question.

(a) Think of AB as the base of this triangle. Measure the base and height, and calculate the area (to the nearest $0 \cdot 1 \, \text{cm}^2$).

(b) Do the same with BC as the base.

(c) Do the same with AC as the base.

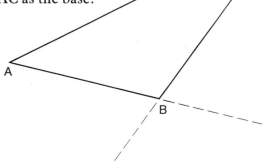

B2 Find the area of each triangle on the worksheet, to the nearest $0 \cdot 1 \, \text{cm}^2$.

B3 (a) Calculate the area, in square units, of the triangle XYZ.

(b) Calculate the area of the triangle with corners at $(^-1, 4), (1, 4)$ and $(0, ^-3)$.

(c) Calculate the area of the triangle with corners at $(3, ^-3), (^-3, 4)$ and $(0, ^-3)$.

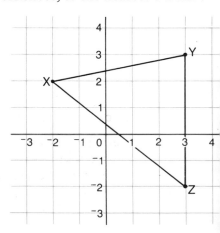

Any shape with straight sides can be split up
into triangles.
So if you know how to find the area of a triangle,
you can find the area of any straight-sided shape.

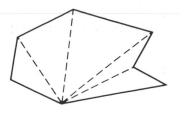

B4 This plan of a piece of building land is drawn to a
scale of 1 cm to 10 m.

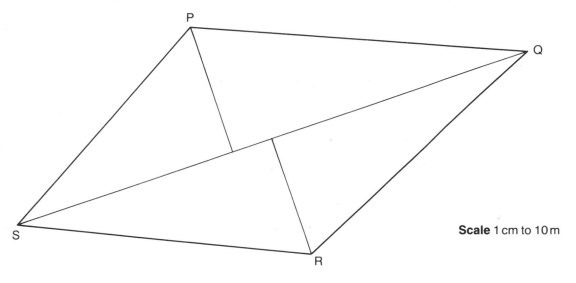

Scale 1 cm to 10 m

(a) Measure the distance SQ on the plan, in centimetres.

(b) What is the real distance SQ, in metres? (Remember that
each centimetre on the plan stands for 10 metres.)

(c) Look at triangle PSQ. Take SQ as the base.
Measure the height of triangle PSQ on the plan.
Write down the real height in metres.

(d) Calculate the area of triangle PSQ, to the nearest m².

(e) Now calculate the area of triangle RSQ in a similar way.

(f) Add the areas of the two triangles together and write down
the area of the whole piece of land.

B5 *You need worksheet R2–3.*

On the worksheet are the plans of three fields, drawn to
a scale of 1 cm to 10 cm.

Calculate the area of each field by drawing a diagonal
to split it into two triangles. (You can draw either diagonal.)
Don't forget to use a set-square to draw the height of each triangle.

c Drawing a triangle given the lengths of its sides

This is a rough sketch of a triangular plot of land.

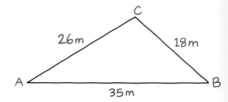

We can make a scale drawing of the plot like this:

1 First choose a scale. Here we shall use 1 cm to 10 m.

2 Choose one side of the triangle and draw it to scale. Here we have drawn the side AB.

A   3·5 cm   B

3 Set the compasses to the length of AC and draw an arc (part of a circle), like this.

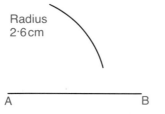

4 Set the compasses to the length of BC and draw another arc, like this.

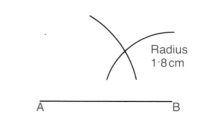

5 Where the two arcs cross is the position of C. Join AC and BC.

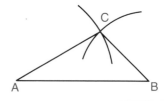

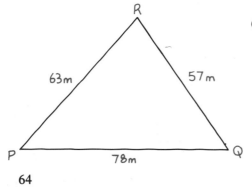

C1   (a) Draw this plot of land to a scale of 1 cm to 10 m.

(b) Choose one side of your triangle as the base. Measure the height at right-angles to the base. Write down the real height in **metres.**

(c) Calculate the area of the plot, to the nearest m².

C2 Draw these triangles, full size, and find their areas.

(a) Triangle PQR, where PQ = 8 cm, QR = 5 cm, PR = 6 cm

(b) Triangle XYZ, where XY = 4 cm, YZ = 7 cm, XZ = 9 cm

C3 A triangle plot of land has sides of length 70 m, 58 m and 64 m.

(a) Choose a suitable scale and draw a plan of the plot.

(b) Is it possible to build a rectangular shed 30 m by 25 m on the plot? If you think it is possible, show where it could go.

(c) Find the area of the plot, to the nearest m².

D The area of a trapezium

A **trapezium** is a quadrilateral with two of its sides parallel to each other.

These are trapeziums:

D1 Which of these shapes are trapeziums?

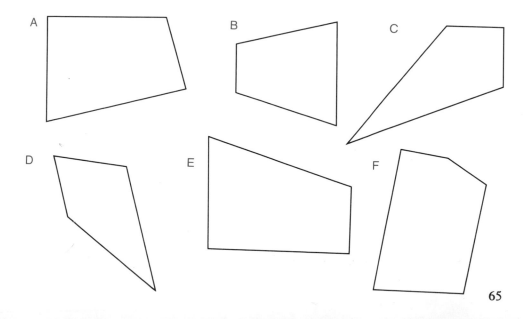

65

Let *a* and *b* be the lengths of the parallel sides of a trapezium.

Let *h* be the distance between the parallel sides, measured at right-angles to them.

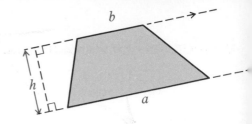

Suppose we have this trapezium, and another one congruent to it (i.e. the same shape and size).

The two trapeziums can be fitted together like this to make a parallelogram.

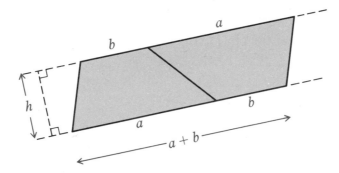

The base of this parallelogram is $a + b$ and the height is h.

So the area of the parallelogram is $(a + b)h$.

To get the area of one trapezium we must divide the area of the parallelogram by 2.

So the area of the trapezium is $\dfrac{(a + b)h}{2}$.

For example, if $a = 7$, $b = 3$ and $h = 6$, then the area of the

trapezium is $\dfrac{(7 + 3) \times 6}{2} = \dfrac{10 \times 6}{2} = \dfrac{60}{2} = 30$.

A very common mistake when using this formula is to forget to divide by 2 at the end. It is therefore safer to do the calculation in this order:

Add *a* and *b* together.	Then divide by 2.	Then multiply by *h*.
$7 + 3 = 10$	$10 \div 2 = 5$	$5 \times 6 = \mathbf{30}$

D2 Use the rule above to calculate the areas of these trapeziums.

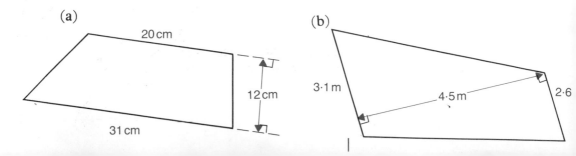

(a)

20 cm

12 cm

31 cm

(b)

3·1 m

4·5 m

2·6

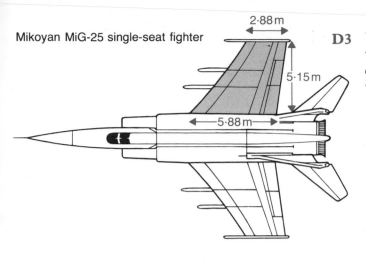

Mikoyan MiG-25 single-seat fighter

2·88m

5·15m

5·88m

D3 Use the information given here to get an estimate of the area of the top of the MiG's wing, to the nearest $0·1\,\text{m}^2$.

D4 This is a drawing of the end wall of a factory.

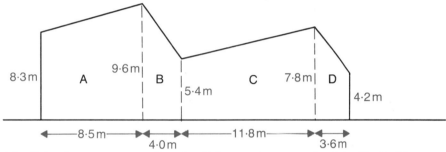

8·3m   A   9·6m   B   5·4m   C   7·8m   D   4·2m

8·5m   4·0m   11·8m   3·6m

(a) Calculate the area of each of the sections marked A, B, C, D.
(b) Calculate the total area of the wall.
(c) Calculate the cost of providing heat insulation for this wall at a rate of £6·50 per square metre.

D5 Find the area of the top of this aircraft's wing (shaded), to the nearest $0·1\,\text{m}^2$.

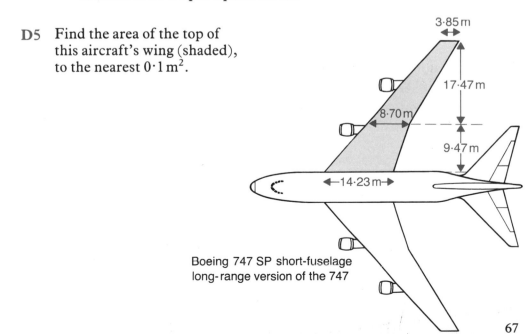

3·85m

17·47m

8·70m

9·47m

14·23m

Boeing 747 SP short-fuselage
long-range version of the 747

An offset survey

For many centuries, probably since farming first began, there have been disputes about who owned pieces of land. So people made maps and plans, as accurately as they could, to show who owned what. When a piece of land was exchanged, or bought and sold, it was necessary to know its area.

Making measurements of a piece of land, and drawing a plan from them, is called **surveying**. There are many different methods of surveying; one of them, described here, is called the **offset** method.

This is how a field is surveyed by the offset method.

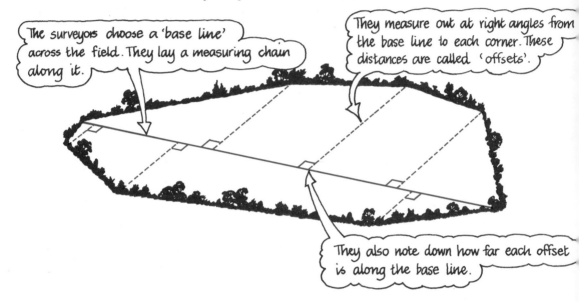

The surveyors choose a 'base line' across the field. They lay a measuring chain along it.

They measure out at right angles from the base line to each corner. These distances are called 'offsets'.

They also note down how far each offset is along the base line.

D6 Here is a sketch-plan of the field.
The numbers marked in red are the offsets, in metres.
The numbers marked in black are distances along the base line, in metres.

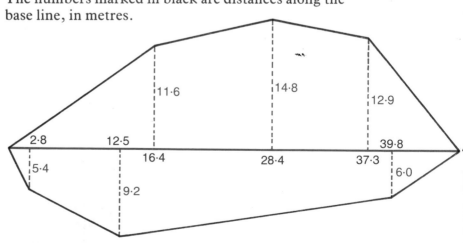

Calculate the area of the field, to the nearest square metre.

12 Proportionality (2)

A Proportionality and graphs

When a motorist buys petrol from a pump,
the cost of the petrol is **proportional** to the
amount bought.

This means that if one person wants twice as
much petrol as another, then the cost is
twice as much. Three times the amount costs
three times as much, and so on.

**When the cost is proportional to the amount, multiplying the amount by
a number means the cost is multiplied by the same number.**

The cost of something is not always proportional
to the amount.

If a large box of detergent contains twice as
much as a small box, it does not follow that
it will cost twice as much. It will usually
cost less than twice as much.

A1 A shop sells lace edging. The cost is proportional to the length.
5 cm of edging costs 8p.

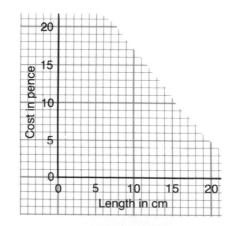

(a) Copy and complete this table of lengths and costs.

Length in cm	0	5	10	15	20	25
Cost in pence	0	8				

(b) Draw axes on graph paper, with
length in cm **across**, and cost in
pence **up**.

Suitable scales are shown here.

Plot the points from the table,
and draw a line through
them.

Here is the graph in question A1.

Length is plotted **across** and cost is plotted **up**.

We shall call this the graph of

(length,   cost)

 across up

(Think of coordinates. When we write (3, 2), we mean 3 **across**, 2 **up**.)

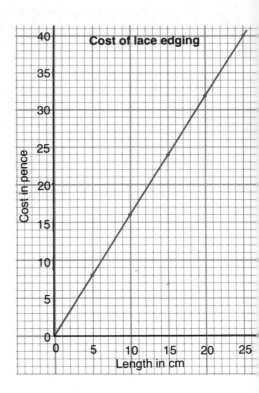

The graph of (length, cost) is a **straight line going through (0, 0)**.

This is the kind of graph you always get when one quantity is **proportional** to another.

A2 The cost of a sheet of hardboard is proportional to its area.

$4\,m^2$ of hardboard costs £3.

(a) Copy and complete this table of areas and costs.

Area in m²	0	4	8	12	16	20	24	28
Cost in £								

(b) Draw a graph of (area, cost). Use these scales:
   Across: 1 cm to $5\,m^2$
   Up: 1 cm to £5

(c) Use your graph to estimate the cost of $25\,m^2$ of hardboard.

A3 If you leave an electric light on for 24 hours, the cost of the electricity is proportional to the power of the lamp. The power is measured in watts.

For a lamp whose power is 100 watts, the cost is 20p.

(a) Draw axes on graph paper, with power in watts **across**, as far as 100, and cost in pence **up**, as far as 20.

Use the scales shown here.

Write the title: 'Cost of burning an electric light for 24 hours'.

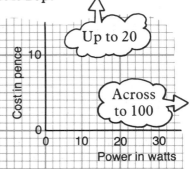

You know that cost is proportional to power. So the graph of (power, cost) will be a straight line through (0, 0).

You know that when the power is 100 watts, the cost is 20p.

Mark the point (100, 20). Draw the straight line through (0, 0) and (100, 20).

(b) Lamps are usually made with powers of 25 watts, 40 watts, 60 watts, 100 watts and 150 watts.

Use the graph to find the cost when the power is

(i) 25 watts (ii) 40 watts (iii) 60 watts

(c) Calculate the cost when the power is 150 watts.

Testing for proportionality

Suppose we have made measurements of two quantities which are related to one another. We can find out if one quantity is proportional to the other by drawing a graph and seeing if it is a straight line through (0, 0).

A4 A student made a pendulum whose length could be varied. She timed 20 swings of the pendulum for various different lengths. Here is a table of her results.

Length in cm	30	40	50	60	80	100
Time in seconds	22·0	25·3	28·3	31·0	35·8	40·0

(a) Draw a graph of (length, time). Use these scales:

Across: 1 cm to 10 cm   Up: 1 cm to 5 seconds

(b) Is the time for 20 swings proportional to the length?

71

B The constant ratio rule

These photos are all enlargements of one another.

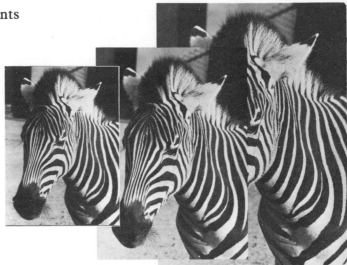

If you multiply the width by a number, . . .

×1·5

Width

Height ×1·5

. . . the height is multiplied by the **same** number, . . .

. . . so the **height** of an enlargement is proportional to the **width**.

B1 (a) Measure the width and height of each photo above, in mm.
Make a table.

Width in mm	
Height in mm	

(b) In the smallest photo, the width is 20 mm and the height 28 mm.

So the ratio $\dfrac{\text{height}}{\text{width}}$ is $\dfrac{28}{20} = 1\cdot4$.

Calculate the ratio $\dfrac{\text{height}}{\text{width}}$ for each of the other photos.

In every photo on the opposite page, the ratio $\frac{\text{height}}{\text{width}}$ is 1·4.

In other words, in every photo the height is 1·4 times the width.

This is an example of the **constant ratio rule** for proportional quantities.

If one quantity is proportional to another, the **ratio** of the two quantities is constant.

Another example occurs in the next question.

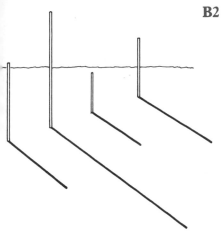

B2 The length of a pole's shadow is proportional to the height of the pole.

Suppose a pole whose height is 5 m casts a shadow 8 m long.

(a) Work out the shadow length for poles of height 10 m, 15 m, 20 m and 25 m.

Height in m	5	10	15	20	25
Shadow length in m	8				

(b) Calculate the ratio $\frac{\text{shadow length}}{\text{height}}$ for each pole.

(c) Use your answer in part (b) to calculate the length of the shadow of a pole of height 13 m.

Testing for proportionality

The constant ratio rule can be used to find out if one quantity is proportional to another.

B3 A student was doing an experiment in electricity. She altered the voltage across a piece of wire and measured the current (in amps) for each different voltage. Here are her results.

Voltage (volts)	8·0	9·5	10·5	13·0	21·5
Current (amps)	19·2	22·8	25·2	31·2	51·6

She wanted to know whether the current is proportional to the voltage. If it is, then the ratio $\frac{\text{current}}{\text{voltage}}$ should be constant.

(a) Calculate the ratio $\frac{\text{current}}{\text{voltage}}$ for each pair of measurements in the table. Is the current proportional to the voltage?

(b) Draw a graph of (voltage, current).

B4 This table shows the weights of copper discs of various different diameters, all cut from the same sheet of copper.

Diameter in mm	12	17	25	31	46	50
Weight in g	0·9	1·7	3·8	5·8	12·7	15·0

(a) Calculate the ratio $\dfrac{\text{weight in g}}{\text{diameter in mm}}$ for each disc.
Is the weight proportional to the diameter?

(b) Draw a graph of (diameter, weight). Suitable scales are shown here.

How can you tell from the graph that the weight is not proportional to the diameter?

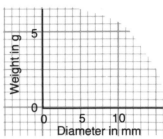

C Gradient

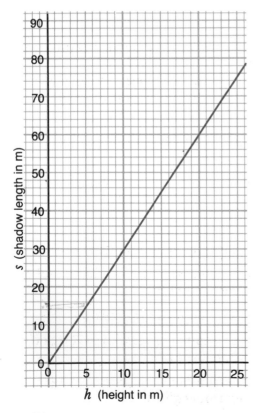

C1 This graph shows the relationship between the height of a pole and the length of its shadow at a time very late in the evening.

(a) Copy and complete this table, using the information in the graph.
h stands for height in metres, and s for shadow length in metres.

h	5	10	15	20	25
s					

(b) Calculate the ratio $\dfrac{s}{h}$ for each pair of numbers in the table.

74

Think how you work out the ratio $\frac{s}{h}$ from the graph in question C1:

Suppose h is 20.

(1) On the graph you go 20 **across**.

(2) Then you go up to find s. It is 60 **up**.

(3) Then you calculate $\frac{60}{20} = 3$.

What you are calculating is the **gradient** of the graph.

The ratio $\frac{s}{h}$ is 3 at every point on the graph. So the **equation** of the graph is $\frac{s}{h} = 3$.

If we multiply both sides of this equation by h, we get
$$s = 3h.$$

This is the most useful form for the equation connecting s and h.

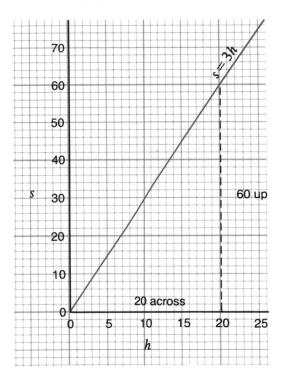

C2 The energy content of foods is measured in calories.
These graphs show the relationship between the energy content, E calories, and the amount, m grams, in two different foods.

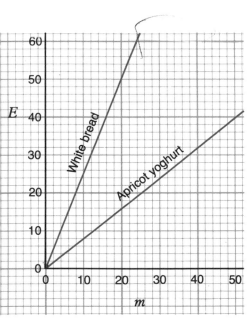

(a) Find the gradient of the graph for white bread.

(b) Write the equation connecting E and m for white bread in the form
$$E = \ldots m.$$

(c) Find the gradient of the other graph.

(d) Write the equation connecting E and m for apricot yoghurt.

(e) Use the equations to calculate

(i) the number of calories in 250 g of white bread

(ii) the number of calories in 250 g of apricot yoghurt

C3 These pictures are all enlargements of one another.

(a) Measure in millimetres the short side, s, and the long side, l, of each picture.
Make a table.

s	
l	

(b) Draw a graph of (s, l).
(c) Is l proportional to s?
(d) Find the gradient of the graph.
(e) Write the equation connecting l and s in the form $l = \ldots s$.

C4 These rectangles are all similar to one another, except for one, which is an 'odd one out'.

(a) Measure the short side, s, and the long side, l, of each rectangle. Make a table of values of s and l.

(b) Draw axes on graph paper, and plot each pair of values as a point. Which rectangle is the 'odd one out'?

(c) Draw the straight line which goes through $(0, 0)$ and the other three points. Find its gradient and write its equation in the form $l = \ldots s$.

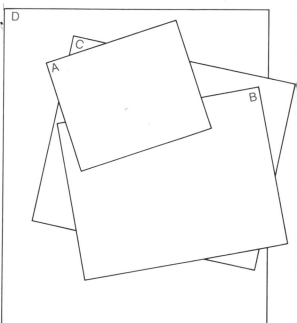

(d) What is the value of $\dfrac{l}{s}$ for the rectangle which is the 'odd one out'?

C5 The length and mass of six pieces of copper wire were measured. Here are the results.

l (length in mm)	20	25	35	55	60	85
m (mass in grams)	44	40	77	88	132	136

The pieces of wire came from two different rolls of wire.
(a) Draw axes and plot the six pairs of values. Each point lies on one of two straight lines through $(0, 0)$. Draw the lines.
(b) Find the equation of each line. Which one represents the thicker wire?

76

D Approximate proportionality

Different masses were hung on a spring, and the extension was measured each time. (The extension is the amount the spring stretches from its original length.)

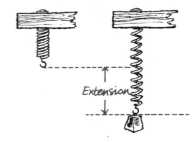

Extension

Here are the results. m stands for the mass in grams, e for the extension in mm.

m	50	100	150	200	250	300
e	80	180	250	350	435	500

When these measurements are plotted, the points do not lie exactly on a straight line through $(0, 0)$.
So e is not exactly proportional to m.

But the points are all very close to the dotted line shown here. This line has been drawn so that it goes through $(0, 0)$ and 'through the middle' of the group of six marked points. Some of the marked points are slightly above the line and some slightly below it.

(The position of the line has to be judged 'by eye'. This means that different people might draw slightly different lines.)

The line's gradient is $1\cdot7$. (You can work it out from the fact that it goes through $(300, 510)$ and $\dfrac{510}{300} = 1\cdot7$.)
So the equation of the line is $e = 1\cdot7\,m$.

The measurements in the table do not fit the equation $e = 1\cdot7\,m$ exactly, but they fit it roughly. Experimental measurements can never be expected to fit a rule exactly.

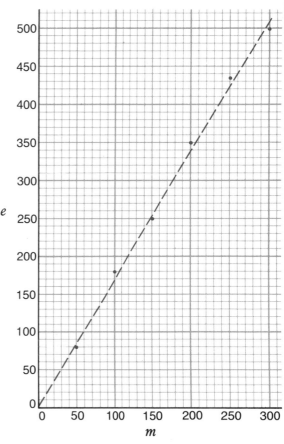

D1 (a) Calculate $\dfrac{e}{m}$ for each pair of values in the table above.

(b) How many values of $\dfrac{e}{m}$ are greater than $1\cdot7$, and how many are less?

D2 These values of m and e were obtained with a different spring.

m	50	100	150	200	250	300
e	60	140	190	270	320	400

(a) Draw axes and plot the six pairs of values.
(b) Draw a straight line through $(0, 0)$ so that all six points are close to it or on it.
(c) Calculate the gradient of your line, and write its equation.

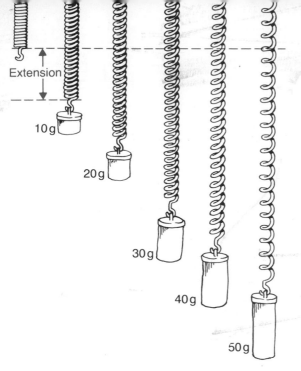

Extension

10g

20g

30g

40g

50g

D3 These diagrams are all full-size. They show the same spring with different weights on it.

(a) Measure in mm the extension of the spring in each diagram. Make a table of values of *m* and

(b) Draw axes and plot the values of *m* and *e* from your table. Draw the line through (0, 0) which seems to you to 'fit' the points most closely.

(c) Calculate the gradient of your line and write down its equation.

D4 These values of two variables *P* and *Q* were obtained in an experiment.

P	1·5	2·1	2·7	3·4	4·0	5·0
Q	0·4	1·5	2·4	3·5	4·6	6·1

(a) Draw axes and plot the values of *P* and *Q*.
(b) Is *Q* approximately proportional to *P*? If so, what equation do *P* and *Q* fit roughly?

D5 This diagram shows distances and single fares (in 1985) from London to some stations on the main line to the south-west.

London	Paddington		
	Slough	18½ miles	£2·30
	Reading	36 miles	£4·30
	Newbury	53 miles	£5·70
	Westbury	95½ miles	£12·40

(a) Draw axes labelled 'distance in miles' across and 'single fare in £' up. Plot the points for the four stations.
(b) Is the fare proportional to the distance?
(c) Which station has the cheapest fare in relation to its distance?
(d) Which has the most expensive fare in relation to its distance?

13 On paper (1)

Do these calculations on paper (or in your head if you can) **without using a calculator**.

1 (a) $417 + 389$ (b) $618 + 43 + 262$ (c) $2683 + 509$
   (d) $£5·86 + £3·05$ (e) $£12·80 + £7·49$ (f) $£58·75 + £26$

2 (a) $372 - 146$ (b) $509 - 268$ (c) $1382 - 773$
   (d) $1600 - 583$ (e) $670 - 264$ (f) $1005 - 377$

3 (a) $761 × 5$ (b) $423 × 4$ (c) $682 × 3$
   (d) $908 × 6$ (e) $537 × 10$ (f) $7 × 234$

4 (a) $364 ÷ 4$ (b) $708 ÷ 3$ (c) $444 ÷ 6$
   (d) $865 ÷ 5$ (e) $1608 ÷ 2$ (f) $2832 ÷ 4$

5 Four people go on a coach trip. The cost is £3·60 each.
   How much does that come to altogether?

6 When I came home from shopping I had £4·83 in my bag.
   When I left home I had £7·50.
   How much did I spend?

7 A customer bought a camera for £26·95. It was faulty, so the
   shop agreed to refund the money. The customer decided to buy
   a different camera, which cost £41·50. How much extra did he
   have to pay?

8 Six people bought a 'winebox' to take to a party. They agreed to
   share the cost equally. The winebox cost £8·70.
   How much did each person pay?

9 Dawn went on a journey for her firm and her firm agreed to
   pay her expenses. Her train fares came to £16·85 and her
   meals to £3·48. What was the total of her expenses?

10 Seven people shared out 468 eggs between them. Each person got
    the same number but some were left over.

    How many did each person get, and how many eggs were
    left over?

14 Plans and elevations

A Getting measurements from drawings

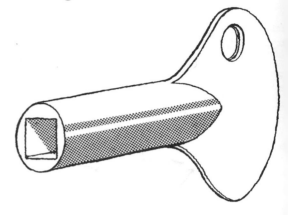

This is a drawing of a key for winding up an old-fashioned clock.

Suppose you wanted someone to make a key just like this one. You would need to give accurate measurements. If a key is not made accurately, it will not fit.

But you cannot get accurate measurements from the drawing. For example, how do you measure the diameter of the shaft?

Is it this . . .   or this . . .   or this?

The drawing above is of no use for measurement.
A locksmith would need to have **views** of the key, drawn full size or to scale.

Here is a side view of the key, also called a **side elevation**.
It is drawn full size here.

A

These dotted lines show the square hole inside the key.

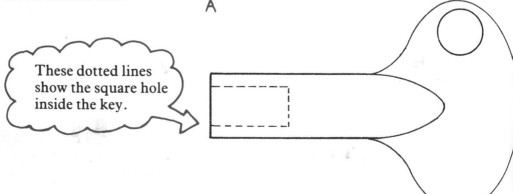

This is an end view, or **end elevation**, of the key.

This is a top view, also called a **plan view**.

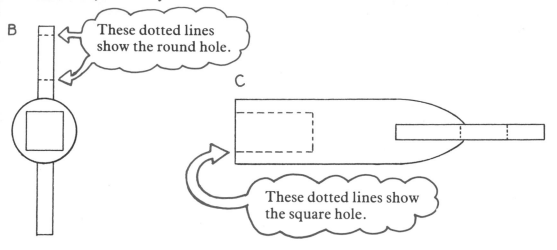

B

These dotted lines show the round hole.

C

These dotted lines show the square hole.

A1 Which of the three drawings, A, B, C, can you measure to find out each of these? (Sometimes you can use more than one drawing.)

Measure them and write down the measurements.

(a) The diameter of the shaft of the key

(b) The depth of the square hole

(c) The diameter of the round hole

(d) The overall length of the key

A2 These are full size drawings of a well-known object.
One is a plan view, the other is a side elevation.

Measure the drawings and draw **full size** an end elevation.
Write the measurements on your drawing.

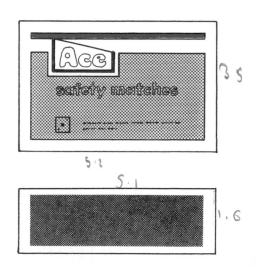

Ace
safety matches

3 5

5·2

5·1

1·6

CAMERA PUZZLE

A3 *You need worksheet R2–4.*

These are drawings of **four** old-fashioned cameras.
There is a plan view, a front elevation and a side elevation of
each camera. All the drawings are to the same scale.

You have to decide which drawings go together and belong to the same
camera. You may need to measure. Use the worksheet for recording
your measurements.

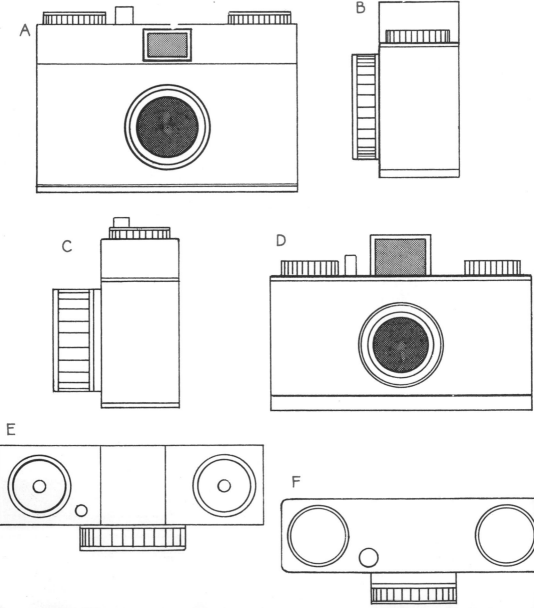

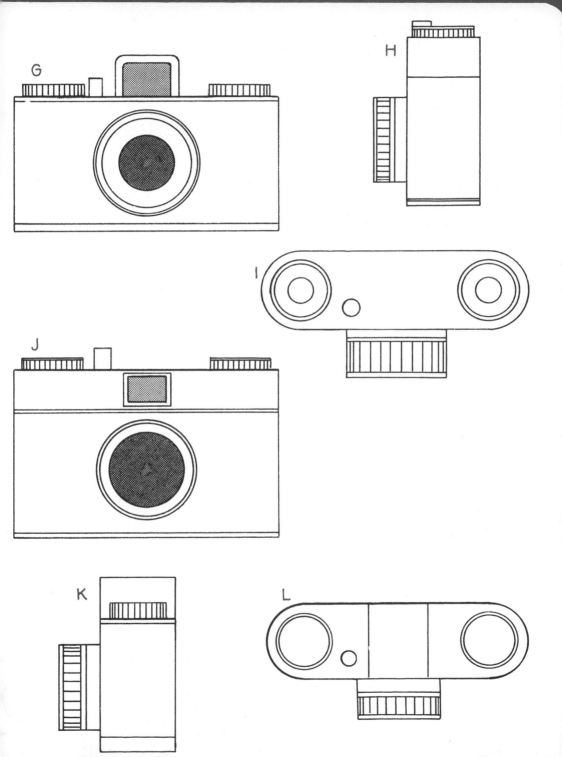

A4 Hema's little sister has seven wooden blocks, all different shapes.
Hema put them on a table, and then drew a plan view, a
front elevation and a side elevation for each block.

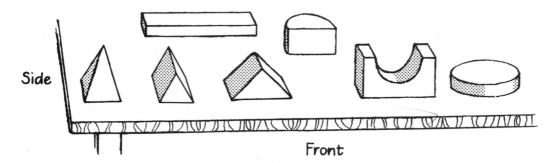

Hema made all her drawings full size. They are shown below
and on the next page. They have got muddled up.

Put the drawings into groups of three. Each group will contain
the plan and two elevations of one of the seven blocks.
Start by picking out the seven plan views. After that you will need
to measure carefully to decide some of the drawings.

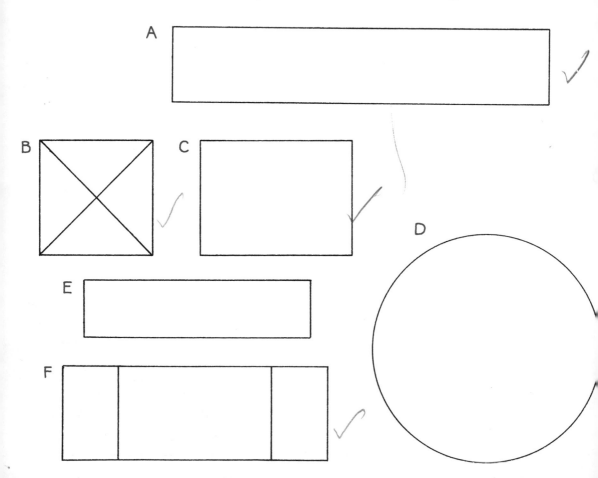

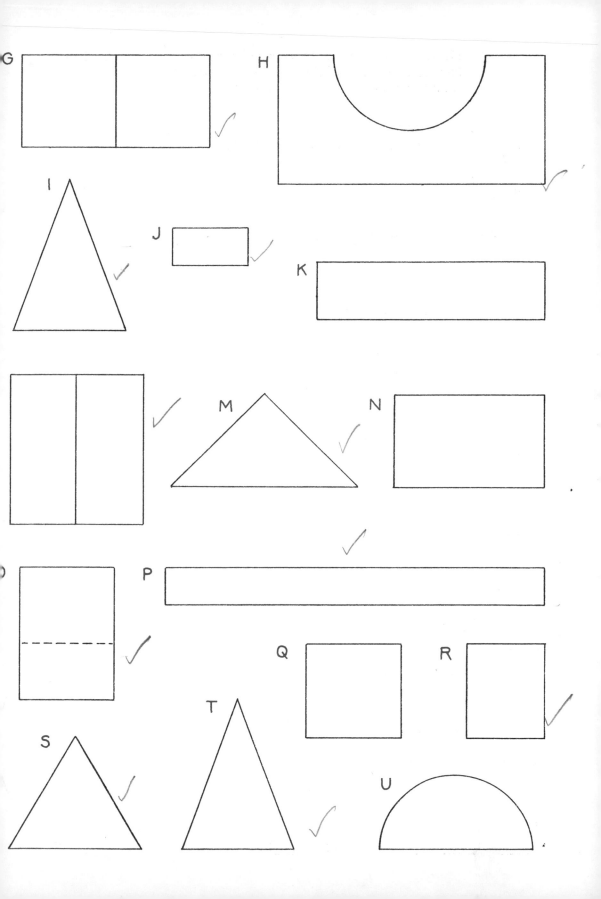

B Buildings

Plans and elevations are often used to give information about the measurements of buildings.

B1 These drawings show a rough sketch of a building, together with a plan view and a side elevation.

The plan and the elevation are drawn to a scale of 1 cm to 1 m.

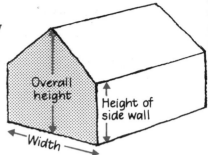

Plan
view

Side
elevation

(a) Which of the two views do you use to measure the width of the building?

(b) Measure the drawing to find the width in metres.

(c) Use one of the views to find the height in metres of each side wall.

(d) Use one of the views to find the overall height of the building.

(e) Use your answers to make a scale drawing of the end wall of the building. (The end wall is coloured in the sketch.)

(f) From your scale drawing, measure the length of the sloping edge of each part of the roof.

(g) Calculate the total area of the roof of the building in m², to 1 d.p.

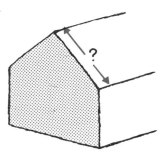

Plan view

B2 These views of a shed are drawn to a scale of 1 cm to 1 m.

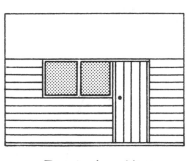

Front elevation

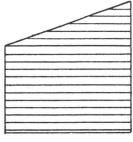

End elevation

Take measurements from the drawings and calculate the area of each of these in m², to 1 d.p.

(a) The floor of the shed   (b) The roof   (c) One end wall

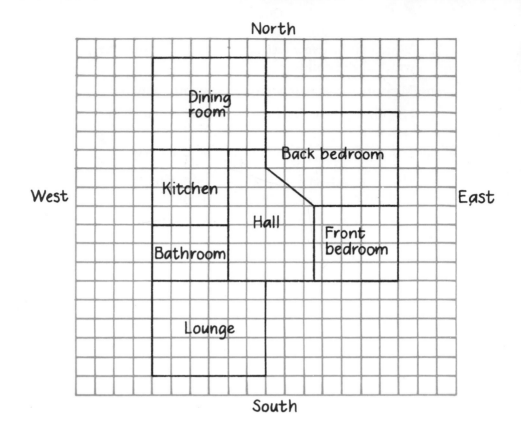

North

West   East

South

B3 The drawing above shows the ground plan of a bungalow.

(a) On the opposite page there are four elevations of the bungalow. Which of them do you see when you look at the bungalow from the north?

(b) Which do you see when you look from the west?

(c) When the artist drew elevation D, he forgot to draw the chimney. Draw a rough sketch to show where it should be drawn.

(d) How many windows are there in the front bedroom?

(e) These drawings show the insides of four of the rooms. Which room is in each drawing?

(i)   (ii)   (iii)   (iv)

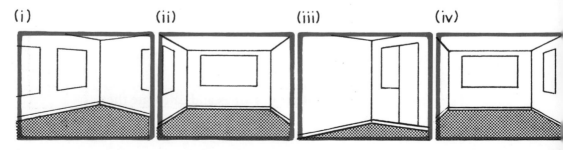

A

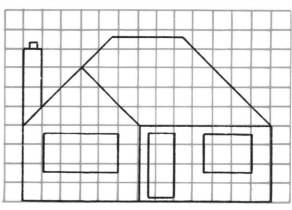

B

C

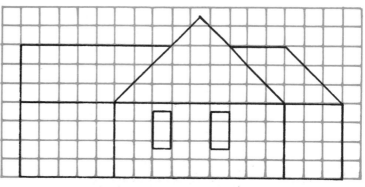

D

15 Rates

A Constant rates

There are two taps in a yard. The first took 6 minutes to fill an 84-litre tank.

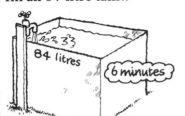

The second took 7 minutes to fill a 105-litre tank.

Which tap is faster?

To answer this, we need find the **rate of flow** of each tap.

We need to find the amo which comes out of each in 1 minute.

For the first tap, divide 84 litres by 6 minutes.
The answer is the rate of flow in **litres per minute**, also written **litre/min**.

For the second tap, divide 105 litres by 7 minutes.

First tap
$$\frac{84 \text{ litres}}{6 \text{ min}} = 14 \text{ litre/min}$$

Second tap
$$\frac{105 \text{ litres}}{7 \text{ min}} = 15 \text{ litre/min}$$

Second is faster.

A1 Calculate the rate of flow of these taps in litre/min, correct to the nearest whole number.
(a) A tap which fills a 40-litre drum in 4 minutes
(b) One which fills a 600-litre tank in 9 minutes
(c) One which takes 17 minutes to fill a 200-litre tank
(d) One which takes 4·5 minutes to fill a 30-litre drum

A2 A fire engine's hose delivers water at 3500 litre/min.
How much water does it deliver in 15 minutes?

A3 A freshwater spring takes 7·5 minutes to fill a 2·5-litre bottle.
What is the rate of flow of the spring in litre/min?

A4 Water comes out of a tap at the rate of 14 litre/min.
(a) Copy and complete this table showing the amount of water which comes out in different times.

Time in minutes	0	0·5	1	1·5	2	3	4	5
Amount in litres	0							

(b) Draw a graph of (time, amount).
(c) Use the graph to find the time this tap will take to fill a tank which can hold 50 litres.

A tap whose rate of flow is constant at 20 litre/min gives a straight-line graph like this.

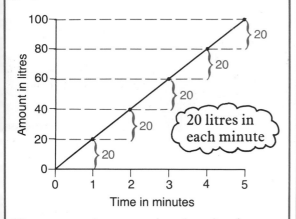

Time in minutes

The amount is proportional to the time, if the rate of flow is constant.

The **gradient** of the graph gives the rate of flow. You must use the scales on the axes to measure up and across.

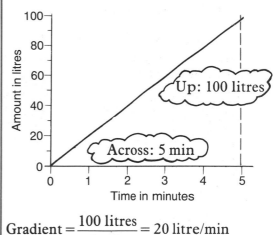

Time in minutes

$$\text{Gradient} = \frac{100 \text{ litres}}{5 \text{ min}} = 20 \text{ litre/min}$$

A5 This graph shows a petrol tank being filled.

What is the rate of filling?

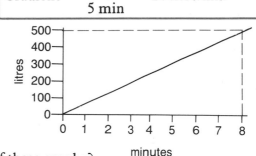

minutes

A6 What is the rate of flow in each of these graphs?

(a)
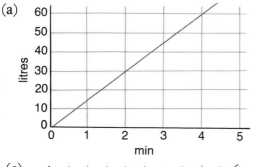
min

(b)

min

(c)
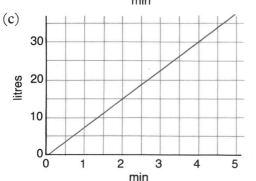
min

(d)
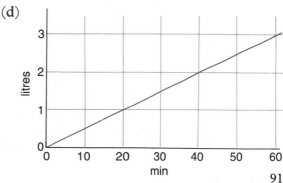
min

If you divide an amount in **litres** by an amount in **minutes**
you get a rate in **litres per minute**.

This works with other units as well.

$$\frac{\text{Amount in £}}{\text{Amount in metres}} = \ldots \text{£ per metre}$$

$$\frac{\text{Amount in grams}}{\text{Amount in cm}} = \ldots \text{grams per cm}$$

3·5 metres of cloth costs £10·15.

$$\frac{£10·15}{3·5\,\text{m}} = £2·90 \text{ per metre}$$

20 cm of wire weighs 2·5 grams.

$$\frac{2·5\,\text{grams}}{20\,\text{cm}} = 0·125 \text{ grams per cm}$$

A7 An aircraft travelling at a constant speed took 23 seconds
to fly 5000 metres.
What was its speed in metres per second, to the nearest whole number?

A8 A machine making plastic tubing spews out 97·5 metres of tubing
in 15 seconds.
At what rate does the tubing come out of the machine?

A9 If £15 is worth the same as $19, work out the exchange rate
between the pound and the dollar (to 2 d.p.)
(a) in dollars per pound   (b) in pounds per dollar

A10 A typist is paid £99 for 36 hours' work.
What is his rate of pay per hour?

A11 A girl who delivers newspapers works for $13\frac{1}{2}$ hours each week
and earns £8·50 a week.
What is her rate of pay per hour (to the nearest penny)?

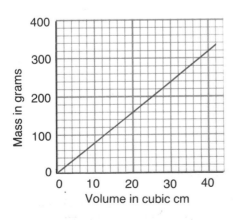

A12 This graph shows how the mass of
a piece of iron is related to its
volume.

(a) Calculate the gradient of the
graph. (Write the units correctly)

(b) What name is given to the quantity
you have just calculated?

A13 The paper on which this book is printed is described as '50 g/m²'.
What does this mean?

B Average rates

The 16:15 train from Edinburgh to London gets to London at 21:15.
It takes 5 hours to cover the distance of 393 miles.

The train does not travel at a constant speed throughout the journey.
Sometimes it speeds up and sometimes it slows down or stops.
If we divide the total distance travelled by the total time taken, the rate
we get is called the **average speed** of the train.

$$\frac{393 \text{ miles}}{5 \text{ hours}} = 78 \cdot 6 \text{ miles per hour (average speed)}$$

B1 In 1960, the 'Flying Scotsman' took 7 hours to go from London to Edinburgh. What was its average speed?

B2 Calculate the average speed of a train which travels from London to Penzance (305 miles) in 6·4 hours.

To calculate a speed in m.p.h. you divide the distance in miles by the time
in hours. If the time is given in hours and minutes, you have to change
the minutes to a decimal of an hour, using the fact that 1 minute = $\frac{1}{60}$ hour.

For example, 13 minutes = $\frac{13}{60}$ hour $(= 13 \div 60)$ = 0·22 hour, to 2 d.p.

B3 Write these in hours, to 2 d.p.
(a) 47 minutes (b) 6 hours 28 minutes (c) 2 hours 7 minutes

B4 From London to Liverpool is 193·5 miles. The 11:50 train from London gets to Liverpool at 14:28. Calculate its average speed.

The average rate of fuel consumption of a car is measured in **litres per 100 km**.
To calculate it you divide the amount of fuel used, in litres, by the
number of **hundreds** of kilometres travelled.

So if a car uses up 13 litres of fuel in travelling 142 km,

$$\text{average fuel consumption rate} = \frac{13 \text{ litres}}{1 \cdot 42 \text{ hundred km}} = 9 \cdot 15 \text{ litre/100 km}$$

B5 What is the average fuel consumption rate of a car which travels 263 km on 30 litres of fuel?

B6 Calculate the average fuel consumption rate of a van which uses 34·6 litres of petrol to travel 180 km.

B7 (a) If 142 km = 1·42 hundred km, what is 86 km in hundred km?
(b) Calculate the average fuel consumption rate of a car which travels 86 km on 10 litres of petrol.
(c) Calculate the average fuel consumption rate of a car which uses 5·3 litres of petrol to travel 58 km.

C Changes in rates

A tap was turned on. Water came out at a constant rate for 3 minutes.

The tap was turned down. Water came out more slowly for 5 minutes.

Then it was turned up slightly, and water came out a little faster for 4 minutes.

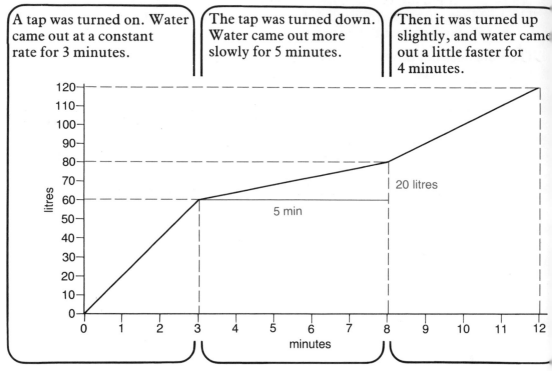

C1 (a) What was the rate of flow during the first 3 minutes?
(b) What was the rate between 3 and 8 minutes?
(c) What was the rate between 8 and 12 minutes?

C2 This is a (time, distance) graph for a train.

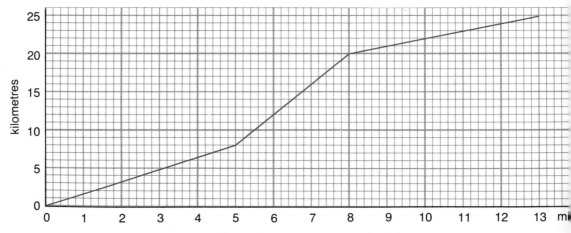

(a) What was the speed of the train, in km/min, during the first 5 minutes?
(b) The gradient of the graph between 5 minutes and 8 minutes gives the speed during that period. What was the speed?
(c) What was the speed between 8 minutes and 13 minutes?

C3 This is a (time, distance) graph for an aircraft.

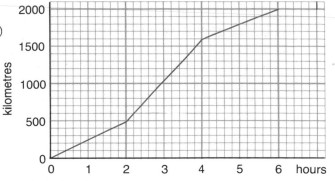

What was the aircraft's speed, in km/h,
(a) from 0 to 2 hours   (b) from 2 to 4 hours   (c) from 4 to 6 hours

The aircraft in question C3 travelled a total distance of 2000 km in a total time of 6 hours.

So its average speed for the whole journey is $\frac{2000}{6}$ = 333 km/h (to the nearest km/h).

The average speed is the gradient of the dotted line.

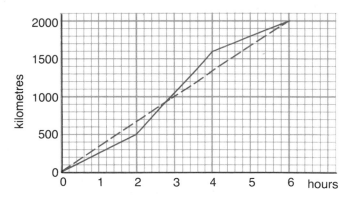

Notice that the average speed is **not** found by adding together the speeds for each part of the journey and dividing by 3.
You have to divide the **total distance** by the **total time**.

C4 Calculate the average speed (to the nearest 0·1 km/min) of the train whose (time, distance) graph is given in question C2.

C5 A car travels at 20 km per hour for 3 hours, and then at 30 km per hour for 4 hours.
(a) How far does it travel altogether?
(b) How many hours does it take for the whole journey?
(c) What is its average speed for the journey?

C6 A train leaves A at 08:00. The map on the left shows when it gets to other stations, and the distance of each station from A.

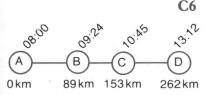

Calculate the average speed of the train between
(a) A and B   (b) B and C   (c) C and D   (d) A and D

95

Some water was heated. This graph shows how its temperature went up.

In the period between 0 and 2 minutes from the start, the temperature went up from 8 °C to 22 °C.

So in that period the temperature rose by 14 degrees in 2 minutes.

So the average rate of increase of the temperature **during that period** was $\dfrac{14 \text{ degrees}}{2 \min}$
= 7 degrees/min.

This means that if the temperature had continued to rise at the same rate, it would have risen 7 degrees in each minute afterwards. But as you can see from the graph, it only rose by 9 degrees between 2 min and 4 min. So in this period the average rate of increase was $\dfrac{9 \text{ degrees}}{2 \min}$ = 4·5 degrees/min.

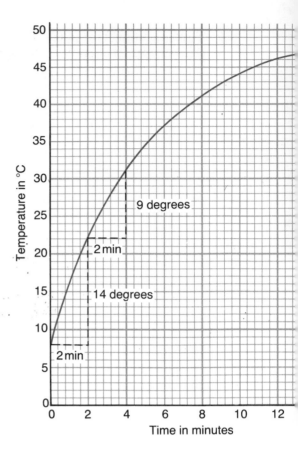

The rate of increase in 'degrees per minute' decreases as time goes on. The temperature continues to go up, but it goes up more and more slowly.

C7 What was the average rate of increase of the temperature, in degrees per minute, in the period between
(a) 4 min and 6 min (b) 6 min and 8 min (c) 8 min and 10 min
(d) 10 min and 12 min (e) 12 min and 14 min

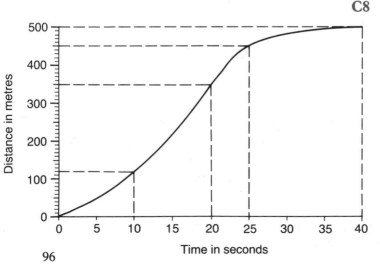

C8 This is the (time, distance) gra for a tramcar travelling betwee two stops 500 metres apart.

(a) How far did the tramcar g between 0 sec and 10 sec?
(b) What was its average spee in m/s during that period?
(c) What was its average spee
(i) between 10 sec and 20 s
(ii) between 20 sec and 25 s
(iii) between 25 sec and 40
(d) What was its overall avera speed for the whole journe

C9 Some liquid is heated and then left to cool.
This graph shows how its temperature changes.

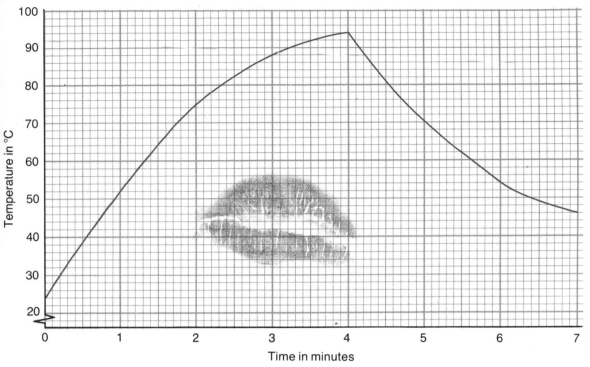

(a) What was the average rate of increase of temperature in degrees per minute between
(i) 0 min and 1·5 min   (ii) 1·5 min and 2 min   (iii) 2 min and 4 min?
(b) What was the average rate of decrease of temperature between
(i) 4 min and 5 min   (ii) 5 min and 5·5 min   (iii) 5·5 min and 7 min?

D Calculations with rates

To find a rate in **litres per minute** you divide an amount in **litres** by an amount in **minutes**. For example, $\dfrac{18 \text{ litres}}{3 \text{ min}} = 6 \text{ litre/min}$.

There are two other types of calculation with rates. Here are examples.

Water flows from a tap at 5 litre/min for 4 minutes. How much water comes out?	Water flows from a tap at 3 litre/min. How long will it take to fill a 24-litre can?
The answer is obviously 20 litres.	The answer is obviously 8 minutes.
5 litre/min × 4 min = 20 litres	$\dfrac{24 \text{ litres}}{3 \text{ litre/min}} = 8 \text{ min}$

D1 A tap flows at 6 litre/min.
(a) How long will it take to fill a 54-litre tank?
(b) How much water comes out of the tap in $4\frac{1}{2}$ minutes?

97

Look carefully at the **pattern** of units.	The same pattern works with any units.
$\dfrac{10 \text{ litres}}{2 \text{ min}} = 5 \text{ litre/min}$	$\dfrac{\ldots \text{ miles}}{\ldots \text{ hours}} = \ldots \text{ mile/hour}$
$3 \text{ litre/min} \times 4 \text{ min} = 12 \text{ litres}$	$\ldots \text{ deg/min} \times \ldots \text{ min} = \ldots \text{ deg}$
$\dfrac{18 \text{ litres}}{6 \text{ litre/min}} = 3 \text{ min}$	$\dfrac{\ldots \text{ m}}{\ldots \text{ m/s}} = \ldots \text{ s}$

D2 How long does it take to travel 156 miles at a speed of 24 m.p.h.?

D3 How long does it take to fill a 34 000-gallon petrol tank at a rate of 8500 gallons per hour?

D4 A sugar solution contains 72·5 g of sugar per litre.
(a) How much sugar is there in 0·80 litre of solution?
(b) How many litres of solution will contain 16 g of sugar?
   (Give your answer correct to the nearest 0·01 litre.)

D5 The electrical resistance of a type of wire is 0·45 ohms per metre.
How many metres of the wire will have a resistance of 63 ohms?

D6 The volume of water in a reservoir has gone down from 18 200 cubic metres to 13 900 cubic metres during the last 7 days.
(a) What is the average rate at which the water has been used, in cubic metres per day (correct to the nearest 100)?
(b) If the water continues to be used up at the same rate, after how many more days will the reservoir be empty?

D7 If a person's heart beats at an average rate of 60 beats per minute, how many times does it beat in a lifetime of 70 years?
(Write your answer in standard index form, to 1 s.f.)

D8 A nurse takes 0·6 litre of a solution containing 80 g of glucose per litre, and mixes it with 1·9 litres of a solution containing 150 g of glucose per litre.

Calculate the number of grams of glucose per litre of the mixture.

D9 A car travelling at 60 km/hour uses up petrol at a rate of 8 litres/100 km.
Calculate the rate of petrol consumption in litres per hour.

D10 A bath can hold 600 litres of water. If it is filled from the cold tap, it takes $2\frac{1}{2}$ minutes to fill. If it is filled from the hot tap, it takes 3 minutes.
How long does it take to fill when both taps are on?

Review 2

10 Formulas and equations (3)

In questions 10.1 and 10.2, round off the answers to 2 significant figures.

10.1 Use the formula $D = \dfrac{M}{V}$ to calculate

   (a) M when $D = 9\cdot5$ and $V = 17\cdot2$

   (b) V when $D = 6\cdot6$ and $M = 48\cdot5$

10.2 Use the formula $F = \dfrac{P}{V}$ to calculate

   (a) V when F is $37\cdot2$ and P is $13\cdot6$

   (b) P when F is $0\cdot85$ and V is $10\cdot3$

10.3 Re-arrange the formula $d = \dfrac{ab}{c}$ to make   (a) a (b) c
the subject.

11 Area

11.1 Calculate the area of each of these shapes.

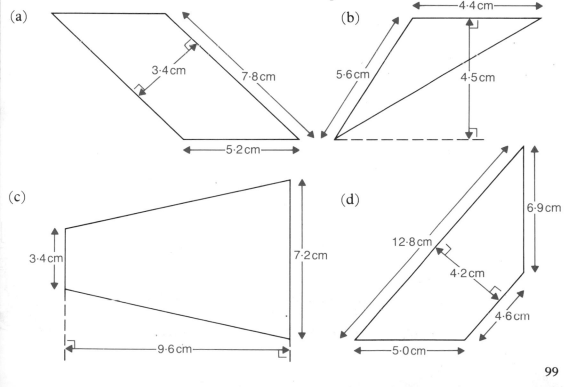

(a)   3·4 cm   7·8 cm   5·2 cm

(b)   4·4 cm   5·6 cm   4·5 cm

(c)   3·4 cm   9·6 cm   7·2 cm

(d)   12·8 cm   4·2 cm   6·9 cm   4·6 cm   5·0 cm

11.2 Calculate the area of this wall.

All measurements are given in metres.

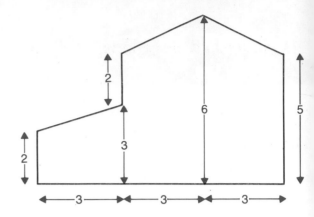

12 Proportionality (2)

12.1 The amount of paint needed to paint a wall is proportional to the area of the wall. A wall of area 65 m² needed 10 litres.

(a) How many litres are needed to cover a wall of area 500 m²? Give your answer to the nearest 0·1 litre.

(b) What area can be painted with 45 litres?

12.2 This graph shows the relationship between two quantities P and Q.

(a) What is the gradient of the graph?

(b) Write the equation connecting P and Q.

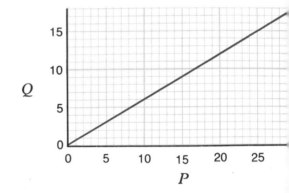

12.3 A student measured the volumes of six pieces of lead and weighed each piece. Here are her results.

Volume in cm³	0·8	1·4	1·8	2·2	2·6	3·0
Mass in grams	9·1	15·9	20·4	26·9	29·5	34·0

(a) Draw axes on graph paper and plot the six points.
(b) The student made an error in measuring either the volume or the mass of one of the pieces of lead. Put a ring round the incorrect point.
(c) Draw the straight line through (0, 0) which best fits the five remaining points.
(d) Calculate the gradient of the line of best fit.
(e) What does the value of the gradient tell you about the lead?

14 Plans and elevations

14.1 There are six different radios shown here. There is a plan view, a front elevation and a side elevation of each one.

Say which views go together as views of the same radio.

14.2 These are drawings of a simple cucumber frame. The shaded part is glass. The scale of the drawings is 1 cm to 10 cm.

Work out the area of the glass.

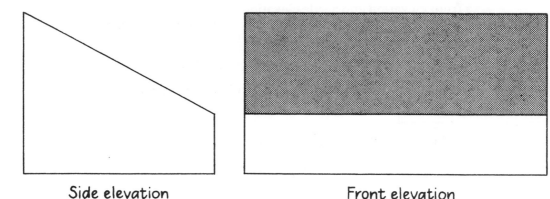

Side elevation   Front elevation

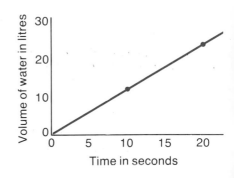

14.3 These drawings show a plan view and a side elevation of a model church.

Sketch an end elevation (left-hand end).

15 Rates

15.1 This graph shows a boiler being filled with water.

Calculate the rate of filling

(a) in litres per second

(b) in litres per minute

15.2   A standard radio battery costs 58p and lasts for 210 hours.
A super battery costs £1·45 and lasts for 650 hours.
Which battery is better value for money? Explain how
you decide.

15.3   In an electro-plating process, copper is deposited at a rate of
31·2 grams per hour.

(a) How much copper is deposited in 10 minutes?

(b) How long will it take to deposit 100 grams of copper, to the
nearest 0·1 hour?

15.4   In May 1985, £1 was worth 1·22 US dollars. It was also
worth 310 Japanese yen. Use these figures to calculate the
exchange rate between the dollar and the yen
(a) in yen per dollar   (b) in dollars per yen

15.5   This is the (time, temperature) graph for a cooling oven.

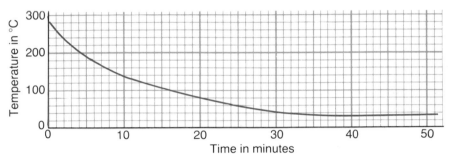

Calculate the average rate of fall of the temperature in deg./min
between   (a) 0 min and 20 min   (b) 20 min and 50 min

M   Miscellaneous

M1   Calculate the sides marked with letters in each of these
right-angled triangles.

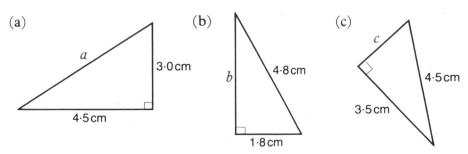

M2   A rail fare goes up from £7·80 to £8·30.
Calculate the percentage increase, to the nearest 1%.

103

16 Simplifying expressions

A Order of adding and subtracting

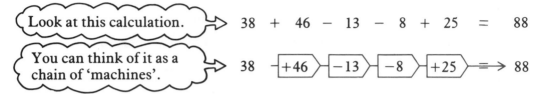

Look at this calculation. $38 + 46 - 13 - 8 + 25 = 88$

You can think of it as a chain of 'machines'. $38 \rightarrow \boxed{+46} \rightarrow \boxed{-13} \rightarrow \boxed{-8} \rightarrow \boxed{+25} \Rightarrow 88$

Each 'machine' is called an **operation**.
In this calculation they are all adding or subtracting operations.

A1 This calculation has the same operations as above, but in a different order.

$38 \rightarrow \boxed{-8} \rightarrow \boxed{+25} \rightarrow \boxed{-13} \rightarrow \boxed{+46} \Rightarrow$

(a) Is the answer the same as before?

(b) Choose another order for the same operations.
Write out your calculation and work out the answer.

$38 \rightarrow \boxed{} \rightarrow \boxed{} \rightarrow \boxed{} \rightarrow \boxed{} \Rightarrow$

(c) Is the answer the same as before?

(d) Choose another different order for the same operations.
(Start with 38 as before.) Do you get the same answer?

Adding and subtracting operations can be done in any order,
without making any difference to the result.

We can use this fact to write equivalent expressions.
For example,

$$a - b + c + d \text{ is equivalent to } a + d - b + c.$$

You can see this by changing the
order of the operations.

Notice that each operation is made
up of a letter (or number) and the
+ or − sign in front of it.

**The signs go with their letters when
you change the order of operations.**

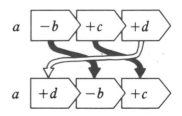

A2 Which of these expressions are equivalent to $w - x - y + z$?

(a) $w - z - y + x$ (b) $w + z - y - x$

(c) $w + x - y - z$ (d) $w - y + z - x$

A3 See how many different expressions you can write down, all starting with w, and all equivalent to $w - x - y + z$.

B Simplifying expressions (1)

This expression is a 'mixture' of letters and numbers.

$$3n - 2 + 4n + 7$$

If we change the order of operations, we can get the n's together, like this.

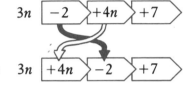

$$= \quad 3n \boxed{+4n} \rangle \boxed{-2} \rangle \boxed{+7} \rangle$$

Now we can go further.

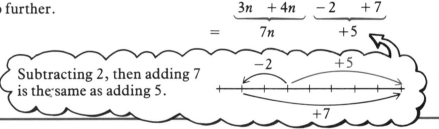

Subtracting 2, then adding 7 is the same as adding 5.

$3n - 2 + 4n + 7$ is equivalent to $7n + 5$.

But $7n + 5$ is a simpler expression.

Going from $3n - 2 + 4n + 7$ to $7n + 5$ is called **simplifying**.

B1 (a) If n is 5, work out the values of $3n - 2 + 4n + 7$ and $7n + 5$, and check that they are the same.

(b) Check that the expressions have the same value when $n = 9$.

We say the expression $3n - 2 + 4n + 7$ has four **terms**.
The **terms** of an expression are linked by $+$ and $-$ signs.
The expression $7n + 5$ has only two terms.

B2 Write down the expression $6n + 3 - 2n + 4$.
Change the order of operations, so that the n's are together.
Simplify the expression.

B3 (a) Simplify $4n - 2 - 5 + 2n$.

   (b) Check that your simpler expression has the same value as this one when n is 10.

B4 Simplify each of these expressions.
Check by replacing n by a number. (Choose your own.)

   (a) $5n + 8 - 2n - 3$ (b) $6n - 4 + 9 + 2n$

   (c) $8n - 3 - 7 + 4n$ (d) $2n - 4 + 6 + 5n$

   (e) $9n - n - 2 - 4$ (f) $7n - 3 + n + 8$

Sometimes the first term is just a number.
Here is an example of this.

$$6 - 2n + 1 + 5n$$
$$= \underbrace{6 + 1} \underbrace{- 2n + 5n}$$
$$= \quad 7 \qquad + 3n$$

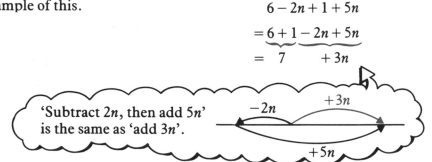

'Subtract $2n$, then add $5n$' is the same as 'add $3n$'.

B5 Simplify each of these expressions.

   (a) $2 + 3n + 5 + 6n$ (b) $5 + 4n - 2 - 2n$ (c) $7 - 2n + 3 + 4n$

   (d) $10 - 2n - 3n + 4$ (e) $8 + n - 6 + 3n$ (f) $9 - 5 - 3n + 4n$

B6 Simplify these expressions.

   (a) $3n - 4 + 2n - 3$ (b) $7 + 5n + 4 - 3n$ (c) $4n - 2n + 6 - 4$

   (d) $3 - 2 - 3n - n$ (e) $8 - n - 3 - n$ (f) $4n - 3 + 8 - n$

B7 Simplify the expression below. The working has been started.

$$3 + 4n - 5 + 2n$$
$$= 3 - 5 + 4n + 2n$$

What is $3 - 5$?

B8 Simplify these expressions.

   (a) $2 + 3n - n - 6$ (b) $4n - 2 - 6n + 7$

   (c) $4p - 5 - 2p + 1$ (d) $6x - 3 - 8x + 4$

   (e) $5 - 3y - 6 + 7y$ (f) $2z - 5 - 6z - 3$

106

c Equations

This equation can be solved by simplifying the left-hand side first.

$$5n - 6 - 2n + 4 = 10$$

First change the order of operations on the left-hand side.

$$5n - 2n - 6 + 4 = 10$$

Then simplify.
Now you have a much simpler equation to solve.

$$3n \qquad -2 = 10$$

C1 (a) Solve the equation $3n - 2 = 10$.

(b) Check that the answer does fit $5n - 6 - 2n + 4 = 10$.

C2 Solve each of these equations by simplifying the left-hand side first. Check each answer.

(a) $2n + 3 + 4n + 1 = 16$ (b) $3n + 5 - 2n - 1 = 7$

(c) $n - 3 + 3n - 5 = 4$ (d) $5n - 3 + 1 - 2n = 7$

(e) $2n + 6n - 9 - 3 = 4$ (f) $8 + 4n - 3 - n = 17$

C3 Solve these equations and check the answers.

(a) $6 - 2n + 1 + 5n = 13$ (b) $10 + n + 2n - 4 = 9$

(c) $13 - 3n + 4n - 2 = 15$ (d) $5n - 6 - 2n - 1 = 5$

C4 Solve these equations. Check the answers.

(a) $5n - 1 - 3n + 9 = 4n$ (b) $10 - 3n + n + 6 = 2n$

C5 This problem comes from an ancient manuscript discovered in India in 1881. The content of the manuscript was originally written in the fourth century AD.

A has something and $1\frac{1}{2}$ extra.
B has 2 times as much as A, and $2\frac{1}{2}$ extra.
C has 3 times as much as B, and $3\frac{1}{2}$ extra.
D has 4 times as much as C, and $4\frac{1}{2}$ extra.

Altogether A, B, C and D have $144\frac{1}{2}$. How much does A have?

To solve the problem, use a letter, for example x, to stand for the 'something' A has.

So A has $x + 1\frac{1}{2}$.

Write down expressions for what B, C and D have.
Write an equation which says that altogether A, B, C and D have $144\frac{1}{2}$.
Solve the equation.

D Simplifying expressions (2)

Suppose we have several numbers multiplied together, for example $3 \times 8 \times 5 \times 2$. Changing the order of the numbers makes no difference to the answer. For example, $3 \times 8 \times 5 \times 2 = 5 \times 8 \times 2 \times 3 = 3 \times 2 \times 5 \times 8$, etc.

We sometimes use this idea in algebra to simplify expressions.

Worked example (1)

Simplify the expression $3a \times 2b$.

$3a \times 2b$ means the same as $3 \times a \times 2 \times b$.

We can change the order to $3 \times 2 \times a \times b$. (Notice that the numbers 3 and 2 come first, then the letters.)

Now we can simplify the expression, like this:

$$3 \times 2 \times a \times b$$
$$= 6 \times ab$$
$$= 6ab.$$

D1 Simplify these expressions.

(a) $4x \times 2y$ (b) $5p \times 2q$ (c) $4a \times 3b$

(d) $4a \times 3b \times c$ (e) $2x \times 3y \times z$ (f) $2p \times 3q \times 2r$

(g) $2a \times b \times 3c$ (h) $x \times 3y \times 5z$ (i) $2a \times 2b \times 2c$

Worked example (2)

Simplify the expression $3p \times 5pq$.

$$
\begin{aligned}
3p \times 5pq &= 3 \times p \times 5 \times p \times q \\
&= 3 \times 5 \times p \times p \times q \quad \text{(changing the order)} \\
&= 15 \times p^2 \times q \\
&= 15p^2q
\end{aligned}
$$

D2 Simplify these expressions.

(a) $2x \times 3x$ (b) $4xy \times 2y$ (c) $3ab \times a$

(d) $5ab \times 4b$ (e) $pq \times 3p$ (f) $4bc \times 5b$

(g) $3ab \times 7b$ (h) $5x \times 4x$ (i) $2pq \times 3q$

★D3 a^2 means $a \times a$, and a^3 means $a \times a \times a$.
So $a^2 \times a^3 = a \times a \times a \times a \times a = a^5$.

Do these in a similar way: (a) $a^3 \times a^4$ (b) $a^5 \times a^3$ (c) $a^6 \times a^4$

What is the rule? Use it to simplify $a^{19} \times a^{27}$.

17 In your head (3)

Decimals, percentages and fractions

Answer these questions in your head, as quickly as possible.

1 (a) $4 \cdot 3 + 0 \cdot 5$ (b) $4 \cdot 7 + 0 \cdot 4$ (c) $6 \cdot 5 + 0 \cdot 8$ (d) $9 \cdot 9 + 0 \cdot 3$

2 (a) $5 \cdot 6 - 0 \cdot 4$ (b) $3 \cdot 1 - 0 \cdot 3$ (c) $4 \cdot 5 - 0 \cdot 7$ (d) $1 \cdot 3 - 0 \cdot 9$

3 What number is halfway between

   (a) 6 and 7   (b) 60 and 61   (c) $31 \cdot 8$ and $31 \cdot 9$ (d) $0 \cdot 5$ and $0 \cdot 6$

   (e) $32 \cdot 9$ and 33   (f) $21 \cdot 92$ and $21 \cdot 93$ (g) 51 and $51 \cdot 1$ (h) 0 and $0 \cdot 1$

4 Round these off to 2 decimal places.

   (a) $7 \cdot 0184$ (b) $24 \cdot 5093$ (c) $0 \cdot 06098$ (d) $124 \cdot 76495$

5 What is 10% of

   (a) £60   (b) £64   (c) £6·40   (d) £8·30   (e) £112·70

6 71 out of 180 is closest to which of these.

   20%   30%   40%   50%   60%   70%   80%

7 If 37% of the children in a school have had chicken-pox, what percentage of the children have not had it?

8 A farmer uses 28% of his land for growing wheat, 45% for growing barley, and the rest for growing oats. What percentage of his land does he use for growing oats?

9 Work these out.

   (a) $\frac{1}{3}$ of 27   (b) $\frac{1}{2}$ of 54   (c) $\frac{1}{2}$ of 92   (d) $\frac{1}{3}$ of 48

   (e) $\frac{2}{3}$ of 54   (f) $\frac{3}{4}$ of 60   (g) $\frac{3}{4}$ of 160   (h) $\frac{1}{5}$ of 75

10 Change each of these to   (i) a decimal   (ii) a percentage

   (a) $\frac{1}{2}$ (b) $\frac{1}{4}$ (c) $\frac{3}{4}$ (d) $\frac{1}{5}$ (e) $\frac{3}{5}$ (f) $\frac{7}{10}$ (g) $\frac{9}{100}$

11 Write these in order of size, smallest first.

   $1 \cdot 06$ $0 \cdot 41$ $0 \cdot 035$ $0 \cdot 57$ $0 \cdot 37$ $0 \cdot 08$ $0 \cdot 308$

18 Contours

A Heights above sea-level

This picture shows an island.

All the points like A, B and C on the coast
of the island are at **sea-level**.

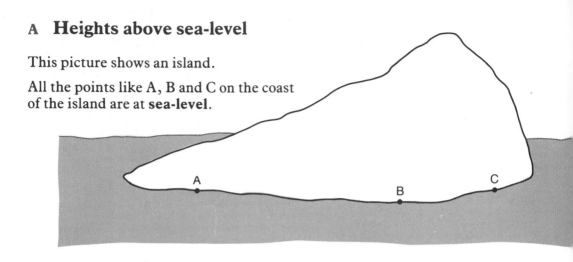

Imagine that the sea rises by 50 metres.
The island will look like this.

All the points on the red line, like D, E and F,
are 50 m above the original sea-level.

The red line is called the **50 m contour**.
It goes right round the island.

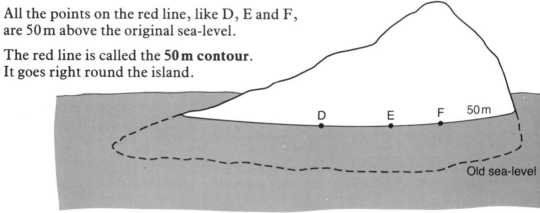

Imagine that the sea rises another 50 m.
We get the **100 m contour**.

All the points on this contour are 100 m
above the original sea-level.

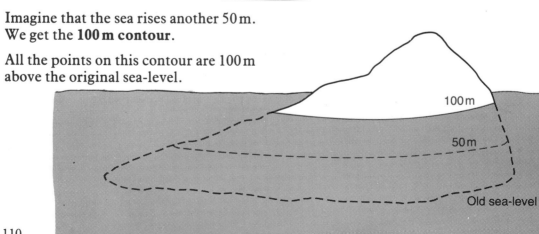

Imagine that the sea rises even further.
This picture shows the 150 m and 200 m contours.

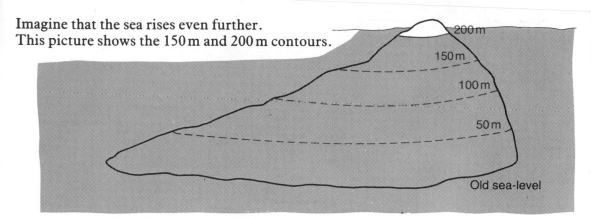

Here is a map of the island, with the sea back at its proper level.
The contours are shown on the map.

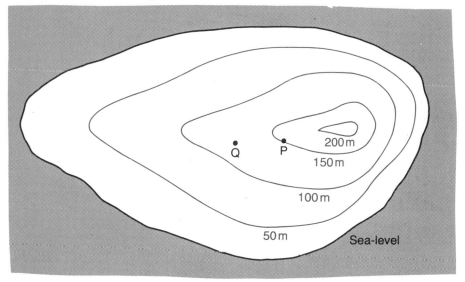

Contours are drawn on maps to show heights above sea-level.
For example, the point P on the map above is on the 150 m contour.
So P is 150 m above sea-level.

The point Q is between the 100 m contour and the 150 m contour.
So the height of Q above sea-level is probably between 100 m and 150 m.

People who use maps a lot can get a good idea of the shapes of hills
and valleys by just looking at contours.

A1   How can you tell from the contours on the map that the
left-hand part of the island is not so steep as the right-hand
part?

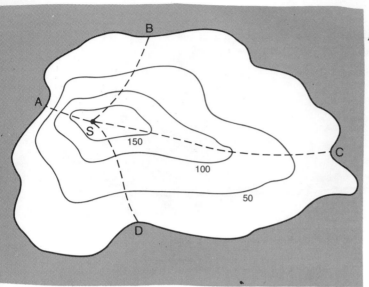

A2 This is a map of another island.

S is the highest point on the island.

There are four paths to S from points on the coast A, B, C and D.

(a) Which is the steepest path up to S?

(b) Which is the least steep of the four paths?

A3 The map below shows part of a country.
The contours show heights above sea-level, in metres.

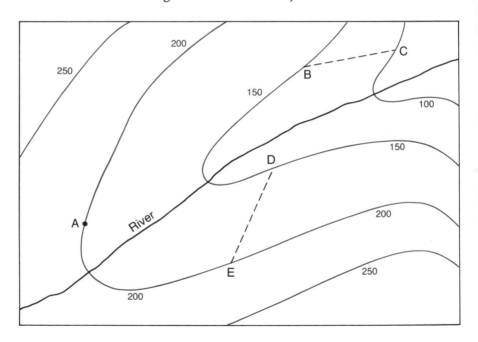

(a) How high above sea-level is the point marked A?

(b) Find B and C on the map. If you walk from B to C, will you be going **uphill** or **downhill**?

(c) Find D and E. If you go from D to E, will you be going uphill or downhill?

(d) Does the river marked on the map flow from left to right across the map, or from right to left?

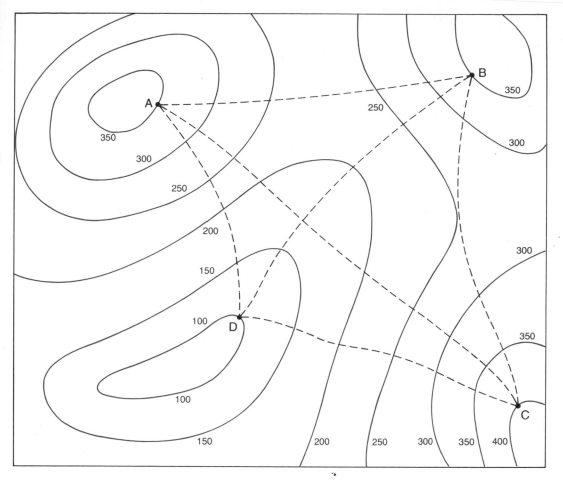

A4 The dotted lines on the map above are paths.

(a) Suppose you start at A and go along the path from A to B. Your height at A is 350 m. Which contour lines do you cross as you go from A to B? Write them down in the order in which you cross them.

(b) Which of these four things do you do as you go from A to B?

Go uphill all the way   Go downhill all the way
Go uphill first, then downhill   Go downhill first, then uphill

A5 Which of the four things listed in question A4 do you do when you go from

(a) B to C   (b) B to D   (c) D to A   (d) C to A   (e) C to D

B Contours on OS maps

This is part of an Ordnance Survey map. The contours show heights in metres above sea-level.

Sometimes the height at a particular spot is marked. For example, in the square whose grid reference is 4843, a spot height of 119 metres is marked.

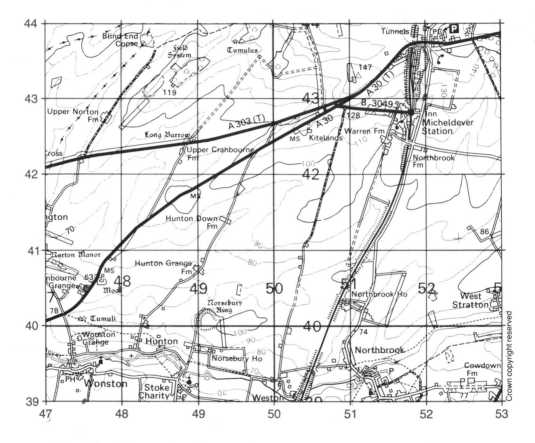

B1 Find Upper Cranbourne Farm on the map. Its grid reference is 488423. What is its height above sea-level?

B2 There is a long barrow near Upper Cranbourne Farm, and a track leads away from it in a north-easterly direction. Starting from the long barrow, does this track go **uphill** or **downhill**?

B3 Find the points whose grid references are 510430 and 475405. Imagine that you are driving along the main road between these two points. How does the road slope? (For example, is it downhill all the way?)

B4 Find Upper Norton Farm (reference 478427). Estimate its height above sea-level.

B5 Find Hunton Grange Farm. Give its grid reference and height.

19 Brackets

A Multiplying out brackets (1)

Let a cm and b cm be the lengths of the sides of a rectangle.

Here are three different ways of working out the perimeter.

Go round the rectangle. Add together the four sides as you go round.	Add together $2 \times a$ and $2 \times b$.	Add together one a and one b. The perimeter is 2 times this.

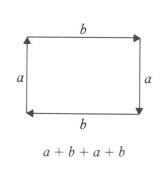

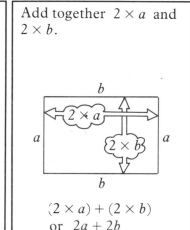

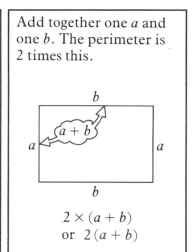

$$a + b + a + b$$

$$(2 \times a) + (2 \times b)$$
$$\text{or } 2a + 2b$$

$$2 \times (a + b)$$
$$\text{or } 2(a + b)$$

A calculation with letters standing for numbers is called an **expression**.

We have three different expressions for the perimeter of the rectangle.

$$a + b + a + b \qquad 2a + 2b \qquad 2(a + b)$$

We say that these three expressions are **equivalent** to each other.
They will always give the same result, no matter what numbers
a and b stand for.

> **A1** Here are three ways of calculating the perimeter of a shape.
> Write down the expression you get for each one.

(a) Add up the sides as you go round the shape.	(b) Think of the shape as made up of 3 long sides and 3 short sides.	(c) Think of the shape as made up of 3 pieces, each consisting of a long side and a short side.

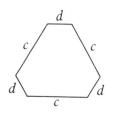

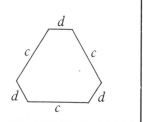

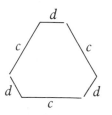

Here are two of the ways of calculating the perimeter in question A1.

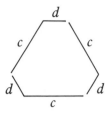   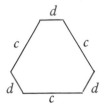

$$3(c + d)$$ $$3c + 3d$$

These two expressions are equivalent, so

$$3(c + d) \ = \ 3c + 3d.$$

Whenever we come across the expression $3(c + d)$, we can replace it by the equivalent expression $3c + 3d$.

Going from $3(c + d)$ to $3c + 3d$ is called **multiplying out** the brackets.

Here are some more examples of multiplying out brackets.

$$2(a + b) = 2a + 2b \qquad 4(x + y) = 4x + 4y \qquad 5(u + v + w) = 5u + 5v + 5w$$

A2 Multiply out the brackets in each of these expressions.

(a) $7(r + s)$ (b) $6(a + b)$ (c) $10(e + f)$ (d) $8(l + m + n)$

'Multiplying out' is sometimes useful when you do calculations in your head.

For example, suppose you want to work out 4×23.

You can think of 23 as $20 + 3$. So 4×23 is the same as $4(20 + 3)$.

When you multiply out, you get $4(20 + 3) = 4 \times 20 + 4 \times 3$
$$= \quad 80 \quad + \quad 12$$
$$= \quad 92$$

A3 Work out 3×57 by thinking of it as $3(50 + 7)$.

A4 Work these out, on paper or in your head.

(a) 5×43 (b) 8×24 (c) 6×32 (d) 4×86

A5 Multiply out the brackets in these expressions.

(a) $5(s + t)$ (b) $2(u + v + w)$ (c) $9(f + g + h + i)$

Look at this 'cross' shape.

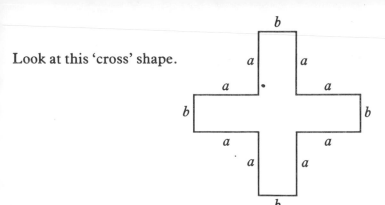

Here are two ways of calculating the perimeter.

<table>
<tr>
<td>

Think of the perimeter as made up of 4 pieces, each of length $2a + b$.

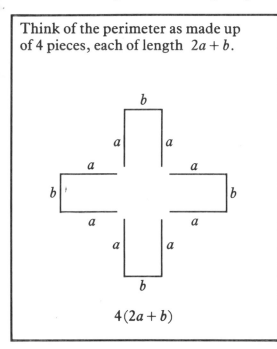

$$4(2a + b)$$

</td>
<td>

Think of the perimeter as made up of 8 pieces of length a, and 4 pieces of length b.

$$8a + 4b$$

</td>
</tr>
</table>

The two expressions are equivalent, so $4(2a + b) = 8a + 4b$.
Notice how the 4 in front of the brackets multiplies the $2a$ and the b.

$$4(2a + b) = 8a + 4b$$

$$\{4 \times 2a\} \; \{4 \times b\}$$

A6 Multiply out the brackets in each of these expressions.

(a) $2(3a + b)$ (b) $5(p + 3q)$ (c) $3(2p + 2q)$

(d) $4(2a + 3b)$ (e) $6(3a + 4b)$ (f) $4(10r + 5s)$

(g) $3(a + 2b + 3c)$ (h) $4(2p + q + 3r)$

(i) $6(5a + 3b + c)$ (j) $8(2a + b + 3c + 4d)$

117

Here is another example of multiplying out.

$$5(3a + 4) = 15a + 20$$

A7 Multiply out the brackets in these expressions.

(a) $3(4x + 2)$ (b) $4(6 + 3p)$ (c) $5(4r + 3)$ (d) $2(7 + 3y)$

(e) $8(a + 5)$ (f) $6(3a + 1)$ (g) $10(3a + 8)$ (h) $7(5 + 2c)$

B Multiplying out brackets (2)

In shops where you buy clothes, many prices have '99p' in them.

If you buy, say, 4 things which cost £2·99 each, there is a quick way to work out the total cost.

£2·99 is 1p less than £3.

True. So what?

4 lots of £2·99 is the same as (4 lots of £3) − (4 lots of 1p).

I see. So that's £12 take away 4p, = £11·96

The method above is an example of multiplying out brackets.

$$4(\boxed{£3} - \boxed{1p}) = 4\boxed{£3} - 4\boxed{1p}$$

Here are some other examples.

$$4(a - b) = 4a - 4b \qquad 5(p - q) = 5p - 5q \qquad 7(u - v - w) = 7u - 7v - 7w$$

B1 Multiply out the brackets in these expressions.

(a) $3(s - t)$ (b) $5(a - b)$ (c) $4(p - q)$

(d) $2(3a - 2)$ (e) $3(5 - 4r)$ (f) $8(2p - 3q)$

(g) $6(a + b - c)$ (h) $5(a - 2b + 3c)$

(i) $4(2a - 3b - 2)$ (j) $10(3a + b - 5)$

C Equations with brackets

I think of a number.

I add 6.

I multiply by 3.

The result is 5 times the number I started with.

Let n stand for the number.

Adding 6 makes $n+6$.

Multiplying by 3 makes $3(n+6)$.

5 times the starting number is $5n$.

So $3(n+6) = 5n$.

To find the starting number we have to solve the equation

$$3(n+6) = 5n$$

The first step is to multiply out the brackets.

$$3n + 18 = 5n$$

C1 Solve the equation $3n + 18 = 5n$.
Check that the answer fits the puzzle.

C2 Solve this number puzzle by solving an equation.

I think of a number. I add 10. I multiply by 4.
The result is 9 times the number I started with.

C3 Solve this puzzle by solving an equation.

I think of a number. I add 18. I multiply by 2.
The result is 5 times the number I started with.

C4 Solve this puzzle by solving an equation.

I think of a number. I add 8. I multiply by 3.
The result is 7 times the number I started with.

C5 Solve these equations by first multiplying out brackets.

(a) $2(n + 5) = 7n$ (b) $8n = 5(n + 6)$

C6 Solve the equation $2(n + 5) = 3n - 4$.

C7 Solve the equation $5(x + 4) = 2x + 35$.

C8 Solve the equation $7(x - 3) = 2(x + 7)$

119

* Problems leading to equations

Sarah is 13 years old. Her mother is 39, which is three times as old. They have a party to celebrate, and enjoy themselves so much that they want to know when next they will be able to celebrate.

This will be when Sarah's mother is twice as old as Sarah.
Suppose this happens in x years' time.
Then Sarah's age will be $13 + x$, and her mother's age will be $39 + x$.

The mother's age has to be twice Sarah's age, so $39 + x = 2(13 + x)$.

*C9   (a) Solve the equation $39 + x = 2(13 + x)$.
(b) How old will Sarah be when her mother is twice as old?

*C10   Olav is 8 years old and his father is 32. They celebrate because the father is four times as old as the son. They can next celebrate when Olav's father is three times as old as Olav.

Suppose this happens in y years' time.
(a) Write down an expression for Olav's age in y years' time.
(b) Write down an expression for his father's age in y years' time.
(c) Write down an equation which says Olav's father will be three times as old as Olav in y years' time.
(d) Solve the equation.
(e) Check your answer.

*C11   Vat A contains 40 litres of wine.
Vat B contains 15 litres.

(a) If x litres of wine are added to each vat, write expressions for
  (i) the number of litres in vat A
  (ii) the number of litres in vat B

(b) After x litres are added to each vat, A contains twice as much as B. Write an equation which says this.

(c) Solve the equation.

(d) Check the answer.

*C12   Repeat question C11, but starting with 50 litres in vat A, and 15 litres in vat B.

D Multiplying out brackets (3)

The rectangle drawn in red has dimensions a and $b + c$.

So its area is $a(b + c)$.

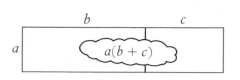

But the same area can be split into two parts, whose areas are ab and ac.

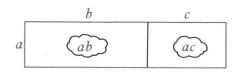

So $a(b + c) = ab + ac$.

Notice that the a outside the brackets multiplies the b and the c.

D1 Multiply out the brackets in each of these expressions.

(a) $x(y + z)$ (b) $f(g - h)$ (c) $s(3 + t)$ (d) $a(p + q - r)$

Worked example

Multiply out the brackets in the expression $a(a - 2b)$.

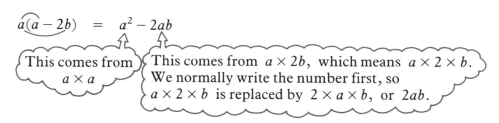

D2 Multiply out the brackets in each of these expressions.

(a) $a(a + 4)$ (b) $x(3 + y)$ (c) $u(v - w)$ (d) $a(b - a)$

(e) $p(p + 3q)$ (f) $r(2r - s)$ (g) $a(2 + a)$ (h) $x(5 - 2x)$

(i) $m(2m + n)$ (j) $x(3x + 1)$ (k) $2a(a + 3b)$ (l) $3x(4 - 3x)$

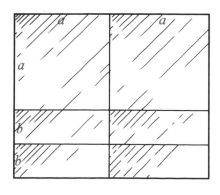

D3 The length of this rectangular window is $2a$.

(a) Write down an expression for the height of the window, using a and b.

(b) Write down an expression for the area of the window, using brackets.

(c) Multiply out the brackets and get another expression for the area.

(d) What does each part of this new expression represent?

121

E Factorising

A large part of the art of algebra is to be able to re-write expressions
in different ways. In the course of a problem, an expression may have to
be re-written several times (without changing its value).

We have seen how to remove the brackets from an expression like $3(a + b)$
The expression $3(a + b)$ is written as the product of two **factors**, 3 and $(a + b)$.
When we remove the brackets we multiply the two factors together and get $3a + 3b$.

Sometimes it is necessary to go the other way and re-write an expression as the
product of factors.
Starting with $3a + 3b$ we rewrite it as $3(a + b)$.
This is called **factorising** the expression $3a + 3b$.

> **E1** Factorise each of these expressions.
> The first is done as an example.
>
>   (a) $5p + 5q = 5(p + q)$ (b) $2a + 2b$ (c) $7x + 7y$
>
>   (d) $9a - 9b$ (e) $4m - 4n$ (f) $3p + 3q - 3r$

Worked example (1)

Factorise the expression $6x + 15$.

> Notice that $6x$ and 15 are both divisible by 3.
> If we have 3 as one factor, then we have to write in brackets whatever
> is needed to make the result equal to $6x + 15$.

$$6x + 15 = 3 (\ldots + \ldots)$$

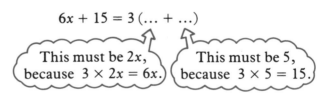

This must be $2x$,
because $3 \times 2x = 6x$.

This must be 5,
because $3 \times 5 = 15$.

> So when we factorise $6x + 15$, we get $3(2x + 5)$.
>
> We can check by multiplying out the brackets: $3(2x + 5) = 6x + 15$.

> **E2** Copy and complete each of these.
>
>   (a) $5x + 10 = 5($)   (b) $9x - 15 = 3($)
>
>   (c) $6a - 8b = 2($)   (d) $30 + 12q = 6($)

> **E3** Factorise each of these expressions.
>
>   (a) $6x + 10$ (b) $9y + 12$ (c) $3p - 30q$
>
>   (d) $14a + 21b$ (e) $8s - 10t$ (f) $6f + 9g$
>
>   (g) $18 - 4q$ (h) $25x + 40y$ (i) $14 + 16p$
>
>   (j) $20 - 5q$ (k) $20x + 15$ (l) $30a - 25b$

122

Worked example (2)

Factorise the expression $12a + 18b$.

Suppose we start by noticing that $12a$ and $18b$ are both divisible by 2.
If we have 2 as one factor, we get this:

$$12a + 18b = 2(6a + 9b)$$

> But this can still be factorised, because $6a$ and $9b$ are both divisible by 3.
>
> $6a + 9b = 3(2a + 3b)$.

So $\quad 12a + 18b = 2 \times 3(2a + 3b)$
$$= 6(2a + 3b)$$

We could have got to this result in one step, if we had noticed that $12a$ and $18b$ are both divisible by 6.

Look for the **largest** factor to go outside the brackets.

E4 Factorise these expressions.
  (a) $4a + 12b$ (b) $20x - 12y$ (c) $6x + 18y$ (d) $12a + 16b$
  (e) $24 + 20p$ (f) $30a - 40$ (g) $8x - 24y$ (h) $28x - 36y$

The factor outside the brackets can include a letter, as in the next example.

Worked example (3)

Factorise the expression $4a + 6ab$.

$4a$ and $6ab$ both have the factor 2, also the factor a.
So we can have $2a$ as one factor.

$$4a + 6ab = 2a(\ldots + \ldots)$$

> This must be 2. This must be $3b$.

E5 Factorise these expressions.

  (a) $2r + rs$ (b) $3a + ab$ (c) $xy + 5x$ (d) $2a + 4ab$

  (e) $6x + 9xy$ (f) $ax + ay$ (g) $5px + 5qy$ (h) $4ax + 6ay$

E6 This is a rectangular animal pen.
The inside wall of the pen has to be painted with a special paint.

  (a) Explain why the total area to be painted is $2lh + 2bh$.

  (b) Factorise this expression.

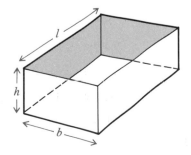

123

20 Probability

A Random selection

Rotating drums like this one are often used to select the winner of a raffle. All the numbered tickets are put into the drum, which is then rotated to mix them all up. Then the drum is opened and someone puts his hand in without looking. He picks out a ticket and reads out the winning number.

Suppose there are 200 tickets inside, numbered 1 to 200.
They are all mixed up, and the person who picks one is not looking.
Every ticket has an equal chance of being chosen.
We call this method of picking a ticket **random selection**.

Now suppose you have bought ticket number 68.
This ticket has 1 chance out of 200 of being the winner.

We write the chance of winning as a fraction, $\frac{1}{200}$, or a decimal, $0\cdot005$.

If you have bought two tickets, your chance of winning is 2 out of 200, or $\frac{2}{200}$, which is equal to $\frac{1}{100}$ or $0\cdot01$.

> **A1** A drum contains 50 tickets numbered 1 to 50.
> One ticket is drawn by random selection from the drum.
> What is your chance of winning if you have bought tickets 36, 37 and 38? Write your answer as a fraction and as a decimal.

> **A2** What is your chance of winning (as a fraction and as a decimal) if you have bought
>
> (a) 1 ticket out of 40
> (b) 7 tickets out of 40
> (c) 7 tickets out of 400
> (d) 3 tickets out of 1000
> (e) 1 ticket out of 65
> (f) 9 tickets out of 65
> (g) 1 ticket out of 100
> (h) 5 tickets out of 500

> **A3** A bowl contains 100 ping-pong balls. Five of them are marked with a spot.
> A person selects a ball 'at random' by putting in his hand without looking, mixing up the balls, and picking one out.
>
> (a) What is the chance of picking out a ball with a spot?
> (b) What is the chance of picking out a ball without a spot?

Random selection does not have to be done by picking something out of a drum or bowl, etc. When you throw an ordinary dice, you are making a random selection of one number out of the six possible numbers 1 to 6.

Each of the six numbers has the same chance of coming up. So the chance of getting a four, say, is $\frac{1}{6}$.

A4 The faces of an ordinary dice are coloured as shown here. (The diagram shows the dice 'opened out' so that you can see every face.)

If the dice is thrown, what is the chance of getting (a) a three (b) a red face (c) a black face

A5 If this spinner is spun, what is the chance of getting

(a) 6 (b) red (c) black (d) white

A6 In a game of bingo, the caller has a bowl, which to start with contains 90 balls, numbered 1 to 90. He selects a ball at random, calls out the number and puts the ball to one side. Then he makes another random selection from those that are left, and so on until the bowl is empty.

Each player has a card with 15 numbers on it and ticks off each number when it is called. The winner is the first to complete a card.

Jane is playing bingo. So far, ten numbers have been called, but none of them is on her card. What is the chance that the next number called is on her card?

Split the class up into pairs for this activity. Each pair needs a dice.

1 Call yourselves A and B.
A marks **either** two faces **or** four faces of the dice with a coloured spot. (Use a felt-tip pen so that it will come off later.) Do not tell B whether two or four faces have been marked.

2 A throws the dice where B cannot see it, and calls out 'yes' if a marked face comes up, and 'no' if not.

3 B keeps a tally of the number of 'yes' and 'no' calls. After 6 throws B guesses how many faces of the dice (two or four) are marked.
A does not tell B whether he or she is right or wrong.

4 After some more throws, B can change the guess, if he or she wants to. Throwing and guessing continue until B feels sure of the number of marked faces on the dice. Only then does A show B the dice.

B Probability

Think of a dice with 4 red faces and 2 black faces.
When the dice is thrown, red is more likely to come up than black.
In fact, red is twice as likely to come up.

The chance, or **probability**, of getting red is $\frac{4}{6}$ or $\frac{2}{3}$, and the
probability of getting black is $\frac{2}{6}$ or $\frac{1}{3}$.

In a very long run of throws, we would expect the number of red to be
about twice the number of black. In other words, we would expect
about $\frac{2}{3}$ of the throws to be red and about $\frac{1}{3}$ black.

> In an earlier book you found the probability that a
> drawing pin lands point upwards, by **experiment**.
> You threw the pin many times and counted the results.
>
> With a dice you can find probabilities by just **looking at it**.
> It is a cube with 6 identical faces, so the probability of each face
> coming up is the same, $\frac{1}{6}$.
>
> You cannot just look at a drawing pin and say what the probability is
> that it will fall point upwards.

B1 A regular tetrahedron has 4 identical faces. Three of them
are red. If the tetrahedron is thrown, what is the probability
that it will land on a red face?

B2 A regular octahedron has 3 red faces and 5 black faces.
If it is rolled, what is the probability that it lands with
a red face on top?

There are 6 ways in which an ordinary dice can fall.
They are called the 6 **equally likely outcomes** for one throw of the dice.
They are, of course, 1, 2, 3, 4, 5, 6.

Suppose you want to know the probability that the number thrown is
greater than 4.
This is the same as the probability that the number is 5 or 6.

'The number thrown is greater than 4' is called an **event**. It is something
which may or may not happen. The outcomes 5 and 6 are said to be
favourable to this event.

The probability of an event is the fraction $\dfrac{\text{Number of favourable outcomes}}{\text{Total number of equally likely outcomes}}$.

When you are calculating the probability of an event, first make a list of
all the equally likely outcomes. Then list or tick off the favourable outcomes.
Then work out the probability. This may seem long-winded at first, but
it will help you to avoid mistakes later.

Worked example

A bag contains four 1p coins, five 2p coins, three 5p coins and three 10p coins.
A coin is drawn at random. What is the probability that its value is
more than 4p?

Equally likely outcomes: 1   1   1   1   2   2   2   2   2   5   5   5   10   10   10
Favourable outcomes: √   √   √   √   √   √

There are 6 favourable outcomes out of 15 equally likely outcomes.
So the probability is $\frac{6}{15} = \frac{2}{5}$.
(Notice that each individual coin is an equally likely outcome.)

B3   In my hand I hold eight cards, numbered 2, 3, 4, 5, 6, 7, 8, 9.
My friend picks a card at random. What is the probability
(a) that he picks a number less than 4
(b) that he picks a number divisible by 3
(c) that he picks a prime number

B4   In Polly's handbag there are six £5 notes, four £10 notes, five £20 notes
and a £50 note, all mixed up. She takes out a note at random.
(a) What is the probability that she takes out more than £10?
(b) What is the probability that she takes out less than £10?

B5   A drum contains 100 raffle tickets numbered 1 to 100. One ticket is
drawn at random. What is the probability that the number drawn is
(a) a one-figure number   (b) a two-figure number
(c) a three-figure number   (d) a four-figure number

B6   In a raffle with 100 tickets, Jack has bought ticket number 58
and Jill has bought ticket number 7.

            Who is right? Explain.

This is a class activity. Each person needs two coins.

Ray: If you throw two coins together, what is the probability that
you get a head and a tail?
Sue: Well. There are 3 outcomes: 2 heads, head-and-tail, 2 tails.
Only one outcome is favourable. So the probability is $\frac{1}{3}$.

Do you agree with Sue? Let each person in the class throw 2 coins many times.
Record the total number of throws and the number of times you get head-and-tail.

c Throwing coins

When you throw two coins you can get 2 heads, head-and-tail, or 2 tails.
But these are **not** equally likely outcomes. You get head-and-tail more
often than either 2 heads or 2 tails.

There is a reason for this. Call the two coins A and B, and think of
all the different ways the two coins can fall. There are 4 ways:

A head, B head   A head, B tail   A tail, B head   A tail, B tail

These are the **4** equally likely outcomes when you throw the two coins.
2 of the outcomes are favourable to the event 'throwing 1 head and 1 tail'.
So the probability of throwing 1 head and 1 tail is $\frac{2}{4}$ or $\frac{1}{2}$.

C1 If two coins are thrown
   (a) what is the probability of getting 2 heads?
   (b) what is the probability of getting 2 tails?

C2 Three coins are thrown. Call them A, B and C.
   (a) Make a list of all the different
       equally likely outcomes. It is
       quicker to make a table, as shown
       on the right.

A	B	C
H	H	H
H	H	T

and so on

   (b) How many of the equally likely outcomes are favourable
       to the event '1 head and 2 tails are thrown'?
   (c) What is the probability of getting 1 head and 2 tails?
   (d) What is the probability of getting 2 heads and 1 tail?
   (e) What is the probability of getting   (i) 3 heads   (ii) 3 tails?

C3 Four coins are thrown.
   (a) Make a list of all the equally likely outcomes. (You will
       find it helpful to start from the list for three coins.)
   (b) What is the probability of getting   (i) 0 heads and 4 tails
       (ii) 1 head and 3 tails   (iii) 2 heads and 2 tails
       (iv) 3 heads and 1 tail   (v) 4 heads and 0 tails

C4 This table shows the number of equally likely outcomes
   when 1, 2, 3, 4 coins are thrown.

Number of coins thrown	1	2	3	4
Number of equally likely outcomes	2	4	8	16

   (a) How many equally likely outcomes are there when 5 coins
       are thrown?
   (b) How many of them are favourable to the event '5 heads
       are thrown'?
   (c) What is the probability of getting 5 heads when 5 coins are thrown?
   (d) A football team has 7 matches to play. What is the probability
       that they will win the toss in all 7 of them?

Throwing two dice

Split the class up into pairs. Each pair needs two dice.

When you throw two dice, the total score can be 2, 3, 4, 5, 6, 7, 8, 9, 10, 11 or 12. Throw two dice several times and count the number of times you get each of the possible total scores. Collect together the results for the whole class.

Which of these frequency graphs do your results look like most?

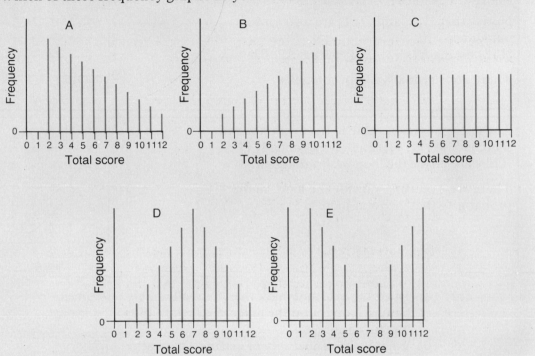

D1 Two dice are thrown. Call them A and B.
  (a) Make a list of all the equally likely outcomes. Write them in a table, as on the right.
  (b) How many equally likely outcomes are there?
  (c) How many of them are favourable to the event 'the total score is 5'?
  (d) What is the probability that the total score is 5?
  (e) How many of the equally likely outcomes are favourable to the event 'the total score is 10'?
  (f) What is the probability that the total score is 10?
  (g) Which total score has the greatest probability? What is the probability of getting that score?

This means 'A comes down 1, B comes down 1'.

A	B
1	1
1	2
1	3
1	4
1	5
1	6
2	1
2	2
2	3
2	4
2	5
2	6
3	1
3	2
3	3
and so on	

129

Look at the list of equally likely outcomes when two dice are thrown.

A	B
1	1
1	2
1	3

You can think of the numbers in the list as coordinates. Each outcome can then be marked as a point on a grid.

Notice that $(1, 2)$ and $(2, 1)$ are different outcomes.
$(1, 2)$ means A1, B2. $(2, 1)$ means A2, B1.

There are 36 equally likely outcomes.

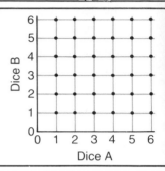

The outcomes favourable to the event 'the total score is 5' are $(1, 4)$, $(2, 3)$, $(3, 2)$ and $(4, 1)$.
They are inside the loop in this diagram.

There are 4 outcomes inside the loop, so the probability that the total score is 5 is $\frac{4}{36}$ (or $\frac{1}{9}$).

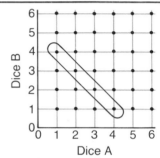

D2 (a) Draw the grid and mark the 36 equally likely outcomes. Draw a loop round the outcomes favourable to the event 'the total score is 7'.

(b) What is the probability of getting a total score of 7?

D3 (a) $(4, 5)$ is one of the outcomes favourable to the event 'the total score is 9'. What are the others?

(b) What is the probability of getting a total score of 9?

D4 Copy and complete this table of probabilities.

Total score with two dice	2	3	4	5	6	7	8	9	10	11	1
Probability				$\frac{4}{36}$							

D5 (a) How many outcomes are favourable to the event 'the total score is greater than 9'?

(b) What is the probability that the total score is greater than 9?

(c) How can you get this probability from the table in question D4?

D6 (a) Draw the grid again and mark the 36 outcomes. Draw a loop round all the outcomes favourable to the event 'the scores on the two dice are equal'.

(b) What is the probability that the scores on the dice are equal?

D7 Instead of looking at the sum of the two scores, we can look at the difference between them.
For the outcome (3, 5), the difference is 2.
For the outcome (5, 3), the difference is also 2.
(Take the smaller score from the larger each time.)
For the outcome (4, 4), the difference is 0.

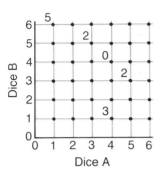

Dice B / Dice A

(a) Draw a grid and mark the 36 outcomes. Against each outcome write the difference for that outcome.

Some of them are shown here.

(b) How many outcomes are favourable to the event 'the difference between the scores is 2'?

(c) What is the probability that the difference is 2?

(d) Find the probability of each other difference and write the results in a table.

Difference between scores on two dice	0	1	2	3	4	5
Probability	6	10	8	6	4	2

E Miscellaneous questions

E1 Peach's Encyclopedia is in three volumes, I, II, and III. Sam takes the three volumes out of a bag at random. He puts them on a shelf in the order in which they come out of the bag.
(a) Make a list of all the different equally likely arrangements of the three volumes on the shelf (for example, I, II, III; II, I, III; etc.).
(b) What is the probability that the three volumes are in the correct order (from left to right)?
(c) What is the probability that volume I is in the correct position?

E2 The four volumes of General Fiasco's memoirs are taken at random and put on a shelf. What is the probability that
(a) volume 4 is in the correct position
(b) volume 3 is in the correct position
(c) volume 1 comes before volume 2 (from left to right)
(d) every volume is in its correct position (from left to right)
(e) volumes 2 and 3 are in their correct positions

E3 Volumes 1 and 2 of General Fiasco's memoirs have red covers and volumes 3 and 4 have blue covers.
If the four volumes are taken at random and put on a shelf, what is the probability that
(a) the two red books are side by side
(b) the two blue books are side by side
(c) the red books are side by side and so are the blue books

21 The circle

A The circumference of a circle

The **circumference** of a circle is the distance all the way round it.

We calculate the circumference by multiplying the diameter by the number π, which is $3 \cdot 141\,59\ldots$

$\qquad$ Circumference $= \pi \times$ diameter

We can shorten this formula to

$\qquad\qquad C = \pi d$

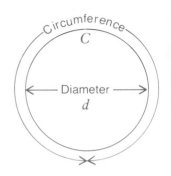

If you do not have a $\boxed{\pi}$ key on your calculator, use the value $3 \cdot 14$ for π.

A1 Calculate, to the nearest $0 \cdot 1$ cm, the circumference of a circle whose diameter is (a) 4 cm (b) $5 \cdot 5$ cm (c) $10 \cdot 8$ cm

A2 (a) How do you calculate the diameter of a circle when you know the circumference?

(b) Sometimes it is difficult to measure the diameter of an object, but easier to measure its circumference.

The distance all the way round this cylindrical tank is $74 \cdot 6$ m.

Calculate the diameter of the tank.

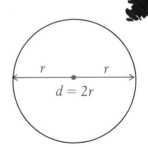

The diameter of a circle is twice its radius.

So instead of $\quad$ Circumference $= \pi \times$ diameter

we can write $\quad$ Circumference $= \pi \times 2 \times$ radius

$\qquad$ or $\quad$ Circumference $= 2 \times \pi \times$ radius.

This formula is written $\qquad C = 2\pi r$

where r stands for the radius.

A3 Use the formula $C = 2\pi r$ to calculate C (to 1 d.p.) when

$\qquad$ (a) $r = 5$ $\qquad$ (b) $r = 6 \cdot 8$ $\qquad$ (c) $r = 31 \cdot 7$

Calculating *r* given *C*

Suppose you are given that $C = 7$ and you want to calculate *r*.

The safest method is to calculate the diameter first, and then divide it by 2.

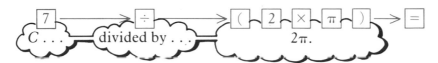

Circumference 7 → ÷ π → diameter 2·228... → ÷ 2 → radius 1·114...

Another method is to re-arrange the formula $C = 2\pi r$ to give *r*:

$$C = 2\pi r$$

Divide both sides by 2π. $$\frac{C}{2\pi} = r$$

If you use a calculator to find *r* from this formula, you need **brackets**:

$$7 \div (2 \times \pi) =$$

C . . . divided by . . . 2π.

If you leave out the brackets, you get this:

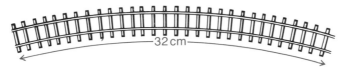

$$7 \div 2 \times \pi =$$

C — This gives $\frac{C}{2}$. — This gives $\frac{C}{2} \times \pi$, or $\frac{C\pi}{2}$, which is wrong.

A4 Calculate, to the nearest 0·1 cm, the radius of a circle whose circumference is
(a) 16·3 cm   (b) 42·0 cm   (c) 38·3 cm   (d) 10·4 cm

A5 A circular model railway track is made up of 12 pieces, each like this:

—32 cm—

Calculate the radius of the circle when all the 12 pieces are fitted together.

A6 An odometer is an instrument used by surveyors for measuring the distances along roads.

The wheel goes round once for every metre the odometer is pushed. Calculate its radius, to the nearest 0·1 cm.

B The area of a circle

This diagram shows a circle whose radius is r.

The area of the coloured square is $r \times r$, or r^2.

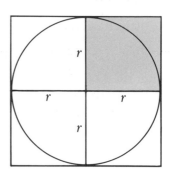

The 4 coloured squares in this diagram
have a total area of $4 \times r^2$, or $4r^2$.

You can see that the area of the circle is
less than $4r^2$.

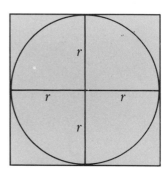

In this diagram, the red triangle is $\frac{1}{2}$ of the
square shown in the first diagram on this page.

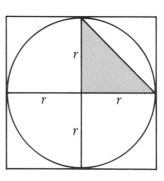

The 4 red triangles in this diagram have the
same area as 2 squares each of area r^2.

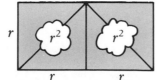

Area $2r^2$

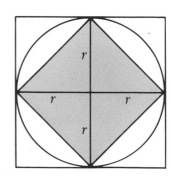

You can see that the area of the circle is
greater than $2r^2$.

So far we have seen that the area of a circle of radius r must be greater than $2r^2$, but less than $4r^2$.

Perhaps the area is $3r^2$? In fact, this formula, $3r^2$, will give quite a good rough answer for the area.

B1 The radius of the circle below is 7 cm.

   (a) Work out the value of $3r^2$ when r is 7. (Remember that $3r^2$ means 3 times (r-squared).)

   (b) Find the area by counting squares. (Squares which are more than half covered have a dot in them.)

   (c) Compare your two answers. Which is larger?

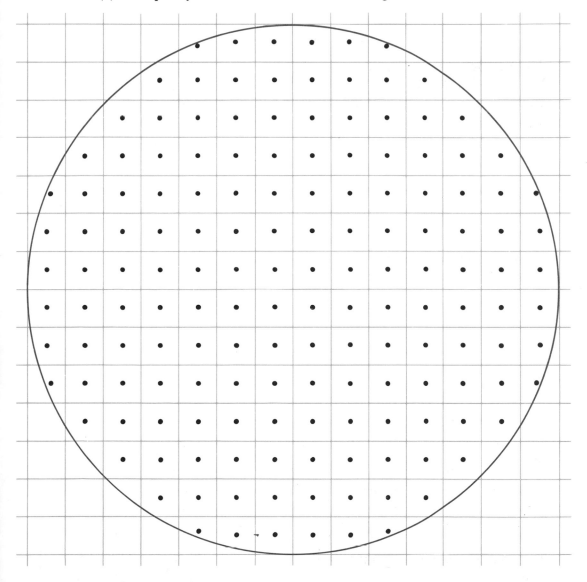

The formula $3r^2$ gives a rough value for the area of a circle.

The correct value is larger than $3r^2$. It is $3\cdot141\,59...\times r^2$, or $\pi \times r^2$.

$$\text{Area of circle} = \pi r^2$$

The diagram below helps to explain why the area is πr^2.
The circle has been split up into pieces which fit together again to make a shape which is almost a rectangle.

The long sides of the 'rectangle' are each half the circumference of the circle. The whole circumference is $2\pi r$, so each long side must be πr.

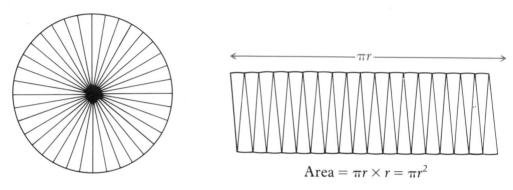

$$\text{Area} = \pi r \times r = \pi r^2$$

Important

πr^2 means π times $\boxed{r\text{-squared}}$, not $\boxed{\pi \text{ times } r}$ squared.

When you use a calculator it is safer to enter the value of r first.
For example, if r is 5, you find the area like this:

$$\boxed{5}\ \boxed{\times}\ \boxed{5}\ \boxed{\times}\ \boxed{\pi}\ \boxed{=}$$

$$\underbrace{}_{r^2}\quad \times \quad \pi$$

If you have a squaring key, usually marked $\boxed{x^2}$, you can enter π first, like this:

$$\boxed{\pi}\ \boxed{\times}\ \boxed{5}\ \boxed{x^2}\ \boxed{=}$$

B2   Calculate the area of each of these circles, to the nearest $0\cdot1\,\text{cm}^2$.

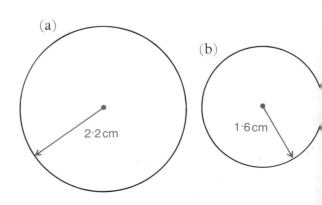

(a)

2·2 cm

(b)

1·6 cm

B3 Calculate, to the nearest $0 \cdot 1 \, cm^2$, the area of a circle of radius

    (a) $1 \cdot 9 \, cm$ (b) $2 \cdot 8 \, cm$ (c) $5 \cdot 9 \, cm$ (d) $8 \cdot 8 \, cm$

B4 (a) Write down the radius of this circle.

    (b) Calculate the area of the circle, to the nearest $0 \cdot 1 \, cm^2$.

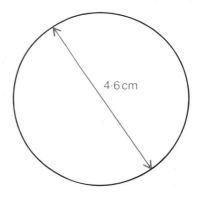

B5 Measure the diameter of each of these circles.
Work out the radius and calculate the area of each circle.

(a)

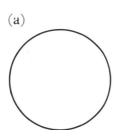

(b)

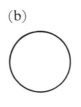

(c)

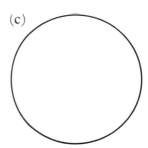

B6 Calculate the area of

    (a) the outer circle, of radius $1 \cdot 6 \, cm$

    (b) the inner circle, of radius $1 \cdot 2 \, cm$

    (c) the shaded space between the two circles

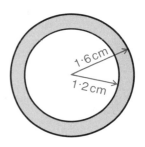

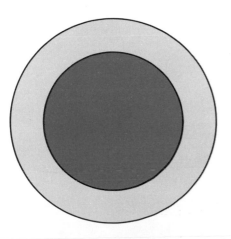

B7 Look at the diagram on the left.

    (a) Do you think the area of the grey ring is greater than, equal to, or less than the area of the red circle?

    (b) Measure the diagram and calculate the area of
        (i) the red circle
        (ii) the grey ring

    (c) Was your answer to (a) correct?

C Mixed questions on circumference and area

C1 (a) Calculate the circumference of a circle of radius 6·8 cm, to the nearest 0·1 cm.

(b) Calculate the area of a circle of radius 6·8 cm, to the nearest 0·1 cm².

C2 Some men on board a ship are marking out a landing pad for helicopters.

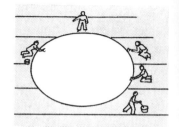

It is a white circle of radius 4·5 m.

(a) What is the area of the landing pad?

(b) What is the diameter of the pad?

(c) What is the distance all the way round the edge of the pad?

C3 Calculate these.

(a) The circumference of a circle of diameter 4·4 cm

(b) The circumference of a circle of radius 8·6 cm

(c) The area of a circle of diameter 12·8 cm

(d) The area of a circle of radius 10·7 cm

(e) The circumference of a circle of radius 6·5 cm

C4 A piece of A4-size paper measures 29·7 cm by 21·0 cm. There are two ways to make a cylindrical tube from a piece of A4 paper, without overlapping.

Calculate the diameter of each tube.

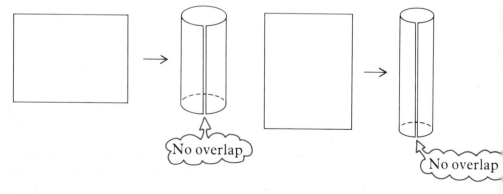

C5 Suppose you have an A4 sheet of paper (29·7 cm by 21·0 cm).

(a) What is the area of the largest circle you could cut out of the sheet?

(b) What area of the sheet is left over?

D The volume of a cylinder

A cylinder is a prism whose cross-section is a circle.

The formula for the volume of any prism is

      Volume of prism = Area of cross-section × Length.

Now we know how to find the area of a circle, we can
also find the volume of a cylinder.

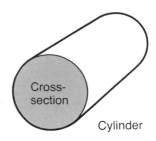

Cross-section

Cylinder

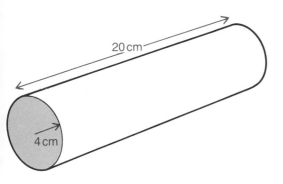

D1 This diagram shows a cylinder whose
radius is 4 cm and whose length
is 20 cm.

    (a) Calculate the area of the
cross-section.

    (b) Calculate the volume of the
cylinder, in cm^3.

D2 Calculate the volume of the cylinders
shown in these diagrams.

(a)

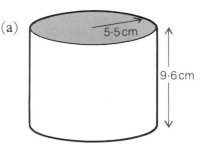

5·5 cm

9·6 cm

(b)

3·2 cm

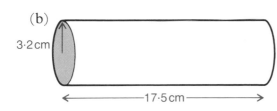

17·5 cm

D3 In this diagram, the **diameter** of the cylinder
is given.

    (a) Write down the radius of the cylinder.

    (b) Calculate the volume.

8·4 cm

7·5 cm

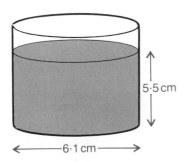

5·5 cm

6·1 cm

D4 The diameter of a cylindrical container is 6·1 cm.
The depth of the liquid in it is 5·5 cm.

Calculate the volume of the liquid.

D5 A pile of ten 10p coins makes a cylinder of height 2·3 cm and diameter 2·8 cm.

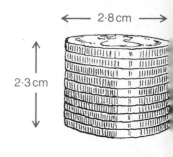

2·8 cm

2·3 cm

(a) Calculate the total volume of the ten coins.

(b) Calculate the volume of one 10p coin.

D6 A single coin is itself a cylinder.

A £1 coin has a diameter of 2·25 cm and a thickness of 0·29 cm.

Calculate its volume.

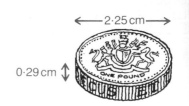

2·25 cm

0·29 cm

D7 There was once a coin called the 'half-crown'. It was 3·2 cm in diameter and 0·2 cm thick, and it was worth $12\frac{1}{2}$p.

Calculate the volume of a half-crown.

D8 The tunnels on London's tube railways have a diameter of 3·7 m. What volume of earth was removed to make a straight tunnel 100 m long?

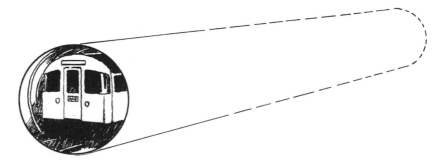

D9 If a litre of water is poured into a glass cylinder of diameter 10 cm, how deep will the water be?

(**Hint.** Calculate the area of the base of the cylinder first.)

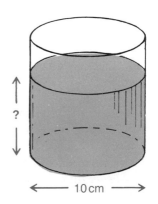

?

10 cm

22 On paper (2)

Do these calculations on paper (or in your head if you can)
without using a calculator.

Try to do them as quickly as you can.

1 A bus company normally has 532 drivers at work, but this week
   185 of them are either sick or on holiday.
   How many drivers are at work this week?

2 A shop sells a skirt for £8·75 and a blouse for £4·85, but if you
   buy both you get the pair for £12·50.
   How much do you save by buying them together instead of separately?

3 A furniture shop sells a table and four chairs for £88.
   The table by itself costs £45. How much do you pay for each
   chair when you buy the table and chairs?

4 I can get six photos on each page of my photo album.
   Altogether I have 36 full pages of photos. How many photos is that?

5 I have to do a business trip from Exeter to Liverpool to Birmingham
   and back to Exeter.
   From Exeter to Liverpool is 235 miles, from Liverpool to Birmingham is
   90 miles, and from Birmingham to Exeter is 162 miles.

   How far have I got to travel altogether?

6 Sandra was paid £20·70 for 6 hours' work.
   How much was that per hour?

7 If you can get 5 glasses of wine from one bottle, how many bottles
   will you need in order to give 85 people 2 glasses each?

8 A shop sells films at £2·88 each, or £16·50 for six.
   (a) How much do you save by buying six films together
        instead of separately?
   (b) What does each film cost when you buy six together?

9 A garage charges £13·50 per hour for labour. What is the
   labour cost of a repair which took 7 hours to do?

10 I have read 173 pages of a book which has 308 pages altogether.
    How many more pages have I got to read?

23 Sampling

A Representative samples

Every so often, especially near to elections and by-elections,
newspapers publish the results of opinion polls.

Here is the result of an opinion poll carried out in a constituency
about a week before a by-election. People were asked which party
they intended to vote for.

**By-election: Labour
narrows the gap.**

The results of the latest opinion poll
put the Conservatives only 5 per cent
ahead of Labour. The full results of
the poll are

Conservative	38 %
Labour	33 %
Liberal/SDP	21 %
Don't know	8 %

The size of the electorate (the total number of people entitled to vote)
was 40 000. It would be very expensive to try to ask everybody, so
the pollsters asked 1000 people how they would vote. The results above
are based on the answers of those 1000 people.

There were 39 000 people who were not asked. So how can the poll
results be of any use in telling us how the whole electorate would
vote?

They can only be useful if the 1000 people are typical, or, as we say,
a **representative sample** of the whole electorate.

It would be no good asking 1000 people who all live in large houses in
the most expensive part of the constituency, or 1000 people who are all
over 70 years old, or 1000 people who are all unemployed. The voting
behaviour of special groups like these may not be typical of the whole
electorate.

Biassed samples

One of the most famous mistakes in opinion sampling was made in the USA in 1936. That year there was an election for president, with two candidates: a Democrat (F.D. Roosevelt) and a Republican (A.E. Landon).

A magazine carried out an opinion poll in which over 2 million people were asked how they would vote. The results seemed to show that the Republican would win easily. But in fact the Democrat won.

The opinion pollsters picked their sample of voters from telephone directories and lists of car owners. At that time, only people who were well-off had a telephone or car, and most well-off people voted Republican. Poorer people, who mostly voted Democrat, were not represented in the sample. We say the sample was **biassed** towards the richer, Republican, voters.

Questions for discussion

A publisher wants to know what percentage of the people in a town read novels. An interviewer is sent out to ask a sample of people whether they have read a novel in the past four weeks.

A1　Why would the interviewer be unlikely to get a representative sample of people if she stands outside the public library and asks people coming out?

A2　Would she be likely to get a representative sample by asking people in the High Street between 10 and 11 a.m. on a weekday? If not, why not?

A3　Suppose she stands outside the railway station and asks people coming home from work. Would she be likely to get a representative sample? If not, why not?

A4　Can you suggest a way in which she could get a representative sample?

B Estimating the size of a population by sampling

You need an ordinary dice.

This is an aerial view of a piece of countryside showing the positions of trees.

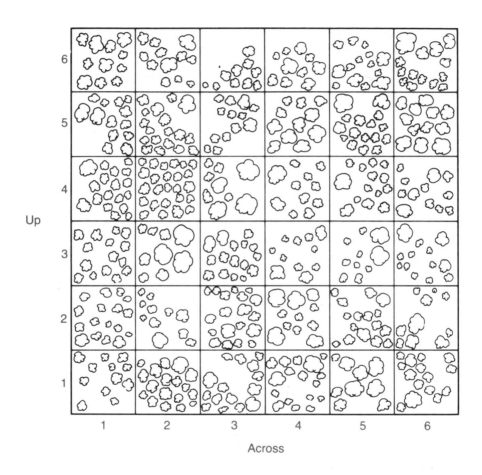

An agriculturalist wants to estimate the total number of trees.
She doesn't have the time (or patience) to count every single tree.

She has divided the area into 36 squares. She wants to estimate the total number of trees by choosing 9 representative squares and counting the trees in those 9 squares. She gets her estimate of the total by multiplying by 4.

B1 Class activity

(a) Each member of the class chooses 9 squares which they think are 'representative' of all the squares. Write down the 'across' and 'up' numbers of each square that you choose.

(b) Count the trees in your 9 squares. (Do not mark the diagram when you count. If you want to mark the trees, put a piece of tracing paper over the diagram.)

(c) Multiply your number of trees by 4, to get your estimate of the total number of trees.

(d) The teacher draws a number line on the board and each person's estimate is marked on it.

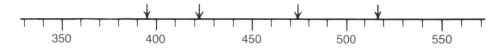

Look at the overall spread of the estimates. Your teacher will tell you what the actual total number of trees is.

(e) Discuss the ways in which people chose their 'representative' samples.

It is not all that easy to choose squares which are 'representative' of all the squares. One way of doing it is to leave the choice to **chance**, so that every square has an equal chance of being chosen to be in the sample.

A sample chosen in this way is called a **random sample**. In random sampling, the choice of sample is decided by tossing coins, throwing dice, or any other way of producing a chance result.

We can choose a random sample of 9 squares by throwing dice. The throws are done in pairs: in each pair, the first throw gives the number **across** and the second throw the number **up**. We carry on throwing until we have chosen 9 squares. (If the same square gets chosen twice, we throw again to get a different square.)

B2 Class activity

Each person uses a dice to get a random sample of 9 squares. Estimate the total number of trees from your sample.

Look at the spread of these estimates and compare it with the previous spread.

Looking at the class's results as a whole, are the estimates obtained by random sampling any worse than those obtained by trying to choose 'representative' squares?

C Using random sequences

This drawing shows part of a collection of felled trees.
There are 100 trees altogether.

Each tree has a reference number. These numbers
go from 00 to 99.

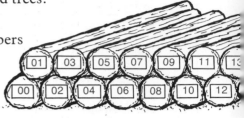

Suppose you want to estimate the total volume of timber in the 100 trees.
It is inconvenient and time-consuming to measure the volume of every
tree, so you are going to choose a random sample of 20 trees.

To understand how this can be done, you need to know about
random sequences.

Random sequences

Imagine a spinner with 10 equal parts, numbered from 0 to 9.
When this spinner is spun again and again, we get a sequence
of digits, for example

   5 0 6 3 7 9 4 7 1 6 5 1 ...

In this sequence it is not possible to predict what the next digit will be.
It is equally likely to be 0, 1, 2, 3, 4, 5, 6, 7, 8 or 9. We call such
a sequence a **random sequence** of digits.

In a very long random sequence of digits, the relative frequency of
each digit is the same. About $\frac{1}{10}$ will be 0, about $\frac{1}{10}$ will be 1, and so on.

Some electronic calculators have a **random number generator** on them,
and most computers can be programmed to generate random digits.
The digits may be produced in groups of two, three or four, for example

  409   789   068   457   449   859   886   213   270 ...

If you do not have a computer, or a calculator capable of generating
random sequences, you can use a **random number table**. This is
just a table of numbers which have been produced by a random
number generator. There is a table of this kind on the opposite page.

How to use a random number table

You can use the table to generate many different random sequences.
You have to decide where to start and what rule to follow for going
through the table. For example, you could decide to

    start at the top right-hand corner of the table, and
    go down the column of single digits and up the next, and so on.

This would give a sequence starting 6 4 5 5 0 2 3 1 2 ...

5568	0813	9599	8781	7973	8801	0529	0060	4049	6477	1818	6321	5996
1570	2557	3603	9014	7268	9575	4471	3283	0521	5984	7320	7848	0614
5392	9184	1587	9829	7587	8451	7862	5077	5683	9062	6982	5722	9495
0282	2355	1630	9600	3494	1785	3437	1136	8557	2139	6532	9081	9835
2784	4079	6617	7649	5164	7169	8351	7303	3814	8156	8224	6239	4950
2848	6085	0016	5328	4591	2931	7557	0680	6782	1311	4861	1825	8102
4236	5293	2612	9972	1876	0309	2511	9500	0750	4930	0501	3833
0421	1509	0166	4833	0972	5984	8486	4816	3981	5635	4077	7131	8071
0697	3993	6510	6562	3127	3206	5709	3722	3271	4458	7487	2819	2772
7426	5641	5306	9213	7695	0360	4146	6075	1573	2914	4406	4045	7770
3117	2065	2957	8777	8113	4243	5186	5530	4552	8780	4093	2222	0079
7992	4354	9030	9163	3384	8334	0713	5966	3315	2931	8004	5741	2703
9737	9507	8963	2469	8676	3540	5132	5927	0139	8917	2272	2971	9118
6292	0501	6793	7425	2791	7831	7833	0214	7858	7046	3268	2960	1569
4298	3588	9412	6191	1451	4694	7662	3585	3867	6988	1616	5162	9188
5922	2767	4329	7878	3908	1288	9550	7976	1554	4763	7157	3713	3336
0019	0364	9448	7794	1799	4694	1530	2245	4507	8156	5165	0993	6250
7725	2356	4228	0747	9293	2972	1402	2226	9373	7008	7955	0872	9353
2247	7495	5486	1989	9966	1065	3017	1506	1978	4541	9156	5275	7878
7507	3723	8208	4632	3393	9290	1089	2540	2318	2979	0611	4528	8370
1680	2231	8846	5418	0498	5245	7071	2597	2268	0932	1882	4466	8450
1958	0382	9064	3511	7001	6239	6110	0613	1180	2624	9274	7598	0050
5417	8950	4530	2895	5605	9740	6827	6130	8353	3203	6493	9449	9206
1736	3480	4995	8567	7469	1505	3499	3957	2237	7623	1323	2943	4795
7630	2759	0496	0472	8906	6029	3547	0198	1369	3492	6785	0730	0001
5420	3648	8794	3712	1533	3950	4341	5840	4200	3840	8523	9025	6138
7920	9186	6596	1243	3426	6852	5140	5044	2807	7905	1860	8934	2387
0873	6060	1720	0047	3582	0639	6730	7649	7505	2484	9261	3539	5832
0899	3037	5554	2229	9341	6729	5380	2443	3650	7521	4615	3188	6012
3629	4605	8125	6880	6463	5349	7979	4525	5958	9010	1808	6708	9884

Estimating the total volume of timber by random sampling

Your teacher has a list of the volumes of each of the 100 trees.
(Of course, in practice these volumes would not be known by anyone,
otherwise sampling would be unnecessary! But the purpose of this work
is to let you see how close your estimates are to the actual total volume.)

C1 Class activity

(a) Each person uses the random number table to produce a random
sequence of 40 digits. Write them in pairs, for example

47   73   12   09   06   64   55   ...

If a pair is repeated, ignore the repeat and continue until
you have 20 different two-digit numbers.

(b) Your 20 numbers are the reference numbers of the trees in
your random sample. Your teacher will read out the volumes
of all the trees. Listen for those trees which are in your sample
and write down their volumes.

(c) Use the information about your sample to estimate the total
volume of the 100 trees.

(d) Mark everybody's estimates on a number line on the board and
compare the estimates with the actual total, which your teacher
will tell you.

D Sampling from a large population

Suppose we want to know the mean height of the fifteen-year-old boys in a school, and we do not have the time to measure every boy. We can choose a sample of the boys, and make an estimate from our sample.

We would want our sample to be representative. A safe way is to choose a random sample. But what should be the size of the sample?

If there are, say, 120 fifteen-year-old boys in the school, would a sample of 10 be sufficient to get a reliable estimate of the mean height? Or is there too great a risk that the 10 boys chosen might include a few exceptionally tall or exceptionally short boys and so be unrepresentative?

In the work which follows you will be finding out in a practical way how reliable sampling can be. You will be taking samples from a very large population of people in order to estimate the mean height, mean weight, etc. of that population.

The actual values of these various means are known to your teacher, so you will be able to find out how reliable are the estimates which you get from your samples.

For the work which follows you need the Database card and the random number table (worksheet R2–5) which goes with it.

The Database card

The Database card contains two databases, called G and B.

Database G contains information about all the fourth-year girls in two neighbouring comprehensive schools.

Database B contains information about all the fourth-year boys in the two schools.

Each girl or boy in each database has a three-digit reference number (from 000 to 194 for the girls, and from 000 to 208 for the boys).

Some of the information is of a simple 'yes-or-no' kind. For example 'can he or she roll their tongue?'[1] In these cases, 1 means 'yes' and 0 'no'.

The measurements of height, waist, etc. are all in centimetres. 'Armspan' means this: 'Handspan' means this:

'Head' means 'head circumference, measured just above the eyebrows'. The weights are in kilograms.

(The information in the databases was collected in February 1983.)

---

[1] This is something people either can or can't do. 'Rolling your tongue' means making it do this.

148

E Estimating a mean

E1 Question for discussion

What size of sample do you think will be necessary to get a reasonably reliable estimate of the mean height of the girls in database G? (There are 195 girls in the database.)

For the next activities you need database G and the random number table. The table has random three-digit numbers from 000 to 249.

E2 Class activity

We will start by seeing what happens when we choose a sample of size 5.

(a) Each person chooses a starting point in the random number table and a rule to follow. He or she then generates a random sample of five different girls' reference numbers.

   (If one of the numbers you get is over 194, ignore it and continue. If you get a number you have already had, ignore that and continue.)

(b) When you have generated your five reference numbers, look up the heights of those five girls in the database.

   Calculate the mean height of your sample. This 'sample mean' is your estimate of the mean height of all the girls in the database.

(c) The teacher draws a scale on the board. Each person's estimate is rounded off to the nearest cm and marked on the scale.

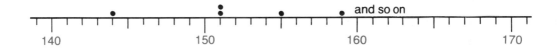

You will probably find that there is quite a lot of variation in the estimates.

(d) Now compare the estimates with the actual mean height of all the girls, which your teacher will tell you.

You may find that some people's estimates were very close to the actual value, but because there is so much variation in the estimates, you could not be very confident about an estimate based on a sample of 5. You might be lucky and get a good estimate, but you would be quite likely to get a really bad one.

Now we will see what happens when the sample size is increased, to 20, say.

E3 Class activity

This time, each person chooses a random sample of size 20. (This can be done by extending the first sample.)

As before, generate your sample first, before you look up the heights.

Calculate the mean height of your sample of 20. This is your estimate of the population mean.

Collect all the estimates together as before.

Is there less variation than before in the estimate?

E4 Class activity

Experiment with other sample sizes.

E5 Individual work

Choose one of the following means, and estimate it by random sampling from database G.

Compare your estimate with the actual mean, which your teacher will tell you.

(a) The mean waist measurement (b) The mean armspan

(c) The mean head circumference (d) The mean weight

F Estimating a median

Imagine that all the girls in database G are arranged in order of weight, lightest first. The weight of the girl who appears halfway along the list (the middle girl) is called the **median** weight of the girls.

We can estimate the median weight by taking a random sample. It is convenient to have an odd number of girls in the sample, for example 21 girls.

F1 Class activity

Each person chooses a random sample of 21 girls.

Look up the weights of the girls in your sample. Arrange the weights in order, lightest first. Find the median weight of your sample. This is your estimate of the population median.

Collect the class's estimates together as before. Compare them with the actual population median.

F2 Individual work

Choose one of the following medians and estimate it by random sampling from database G.

Compare your estimate with the actual median.

(a) The median height

(b) The median armspan

(c) The median waist measurement

(d) The median head circumference

G Estimating a percentage

G1 Question for discussion

What size of sample do you think will give a reasonably reliable estimate of the percentage of the boys in database B who wear glasses?

For the next activities you need database B and the random number table.

Note: You cannot 're-use' a random sample of the **girls'** reference numbers as your sample of **boys**, because the total number of boys in database B is different from the total number of girls in database G. If the girls' numbers were simply re-used, then the boys with reference numbers 195 to 208 would have no chance of being in the sample, so the sample would not be a truly random one.

G2 Class activity

Each person chooses a random sample of 5 boys, and finds out how many of those 5 boys wear glasses.
Write down the percentage of your sample who wear glasses.

If we choose a sample of size 5, the number of boys in the sample who wear glasses can only be 0, 1, 2, 3, 4, or 5. So the estimate of the percentage wearing glasses can only be 0%, 20%, 40%, 60%, 80% or 100%. So samples of size 5 are not very useful for estimating percentates.

We will now see what results we get from a larger sample, say 20 again.

G3 Class activity

Repeat G2 with samples of size 20. Collect together the class's estimates, and look at their distribution.
Compare them with the actual percentage, which your teacher knows.

G4 Individual work

Choose one of the 'yes-or-no' columns in database B, and estimate the percentage of 'yes' entries by sampling. Compare your estimate with the actual percentage, which your teacher knows.

H Scatter diagrams

For the activities in this section we shall use a different method of choosing the sample, based on the days of the month on which people were born.

There is no reason to suppose that people born on a particular day of the month, say the 15th, are in any way different from others. So those born on a particular day of the month are a representative sample of the population as a whole.

H1 Class activity

Is there any relation between height and shoe size among the boys in database B? We shall try to answer this question by sampling.

(a) Each person in the class is given a different set of five days of the month. (For example, 2nd, 5th, 6th, 10th, 28th.)

Note down the height and shoe size of each boy born on any of your five days of the month.

Plot each pair of values as a point on a diagram, like this. This kind of diagram is called a **scatter diagram**. (Don't try to join up the points!)

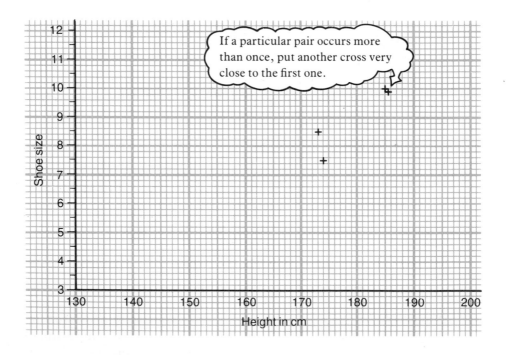

Scatter diagram of height and shoe size

(b) Does your diagram appear to show any relationship between height and shoe size?
(For example, does it appear to show that tall boys tend to have big feet and short boys small feet?)

If so, what feature of the diagram seems to show the relationship?

(c) Compare your scatter diagram with those of other people in the class.

Up to now each member of the class has generated their own sample and compared their results with others.

For the next activity, the method will be different. Only one sample will be generated, and as it grows in size a clearer and clearer picture will emerge.

H2 Class activity

Do tall girls tend to have large armspans?

(a) Each person in the class is given one day of the month. He or she looks up in database G to find the heights and armspans of all the girls born on that day of the month.

(b) Everybody draws the axes of a scatter diagram on graph paper.
Across: height, from 140 cm to 190 cm
Up: armspan, from 140 cm to 190 cm

(c) Each person then reads out the height and armspan of each of the girls in their sample. Everybody plots the points on their scatter diagrams.

Stop when you think you have enough information to answer the question: do tall girls tend to have large armspans and short girls small armspans?

H3 Individual work

Take a sample of either boys or girls from one of the databases.
Draw scatter diagrams for some of the following, and comment on them.

(a) Shoe size, height   (b) Shoe size, armspan

(c) Shoe size, weight   (d) Shoe size, handspan

(e) Height, armspan   (f) Height, waist

(g) Weight, armspan   (h) Weight, handspan

(i) Waist, weight

Review 3

16 Simplifying expressions

16.1 Simplify these expressions.

(a) $3x - 5 - x + 9$

(b) $2 - 8x + 4x + 4$

(c) $3a + 5 - 8a + 1$

(d) $10 - 3b - 4 - 5b$

16.2 Solve these equations.

(a) $3x - 5 + 2x + 4 = 14$

(b) $9 - 3x + 6 - x = x$

16.3 Simplify these expressions.

(a) $3a \times 4b$ (b) $2x \times 6x$ (c) $5p \times 7pq$ (d) $2c \times 8bc$

18 Contours

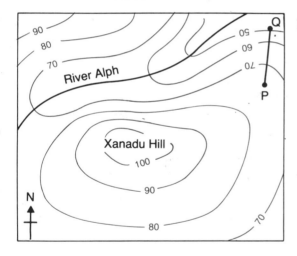

18.1 The contours on this map show height in metres above sea-level.

(a) Which side of Xanadu Hill is the steepest? Is it the north side, the south side, the east side or the west side?

(b) Does the River Alph flow from left to right on the map, or from right to left?

(c) Does the road from P to Q slope upwards or downwards?

19 Brackets

19.1 Multiply out the brackets in these expressions

(a) $5(3a - 4)$ (b) $3(6a + 2)$ (c) $10(8 - 3b)$ (d) $8(5 + 4x)$

19.2 Solve each of these equations. Check each answer.

(a) $x + 7 = 4(x - 5)$

(b) $3(x + 2) = 5x - 7$

(c) $4(2x - 1) = 3x + 11$

(d) $6x = 5(x - 2)$

19.3 Multiply out the brackets in these expressions.

(a) $e(f-g)$ (b) $2a(b+3)$ (c) $3h(h-j)$ (d) $4x(x-5y)$

19.4 Factorise each of these expressions.

(a) $6x+6y$ (b) $5a+20b$ (c) $12x-16y$ (d) $ah+ak$

(e) $5a-ab$ (f) $3nx+4n$ (g) $3ax+3bx$ (h) a^2-ab

*19.5 Janet and John had the same amount of money each. Janet gave John £7. Afterwards John had 5 times as much as Janet.

Let £x be the amount each one had to start with.

(a) Write down an expression for the amount John had after Janet had given him £7.
(b) Write an expression for the amount Janet had left.
(c) Write an equation which says that afterwards John's amount was 5 times Janet's.
(d) Solve the equation. Check that the answer fits the problem.

20 Probability

20.1 Janet has these cards in her hand:

Ace of spades, Ace of hearts, Queen of clubs, Jack of hearts, 10 of hearts, 7 of clubs, 6 of clubs, 6 of diamonds, 3 of spades, 3 of hearts, 3 of diamonds, 2 of diamonds.

Sandra takes one card at random. What is the probability that it is
(a) an ace   (b) a spade   (c) the Queen of clubs   (d) a 3   (e) a diamond

20.2 Two five-sided spinners are each numbered 1 to 5.
(a) Draw a grid and mark points on it to show all the equally likely outcomes when both spinners are spun.
(b) Draw a loop round all the outcomes for which the total score is more than 5.
(c) What is the probability that the total score is more than 5?

21 The circle

21.1 Calculate the circumference of a circle whose radius is $8 \cdot 5$ cm. Give your answer to the nearest $0 \cdot 1$ cm.

21.2 Calculate the area (to the nearest $0 \cdot 1$ cm^2) of a circle
(a) of radius $5 \cdot 3$ cm   (b) of diameter $8 \cdot 3$ cm

21.3 A cylindrical lift-shaft at a tube station has a diameter of 7·4 m. The shift is 24·3 m deep.

(a) Calculate the area of the cross-section of the shaft.

(b) Calculate the volume of earth which had to be removed to make the shaft.

21.4 A circular pond is 45·3 m in circumference. Calculate
(a) its diameter   (b) its area

M Miscellaneous

M1 A couple wish to cover the floor of a rectangular room 5·8 m by 3·4 m with plain carpet.
They think that the cheapest way to do it is to buy a 'remnant', which is a rectangular piece of carpet they can cut up.

The shop has three remnants in stock.
    A is 5·5 m by 4·2 m and costs £110.
    B is 4·9 m by 3·7 m and costs £90.
    C is 8·2 m by 2·5 m and costs £90.

(a) Which remnant is made from the most expensive material?
(b) Which is made from the cheapest material?
(c) Which remnants could be used to carpet their room?
(d) Show how each of these could be cut. It is best to have as few cuts as possible in the carpet on the floor.

M2 The Earth moves round the sun in an approximately circular orbit, the radius being about $9·3 \times 10^5$ miles. One complete revolution takes $365\frac{1}{4}$ days.

Calculate the average speed in m.p.h. of the Earth in its orbit, to 2 s.f. Set out your working clearly.

M3 The area of a rectangle is 30 cm^2 and the length of the rectangle is 2 cm more than its width. If w cm is the width, then $w(w + 2) = 30$.

w

$w + 2$ 30 cm^2

(a) Explain why w must be somewhere between 4 and 5.

(b) Use a decimal search to find the value of w. correct to 1 d.p.

M4 Neeta cycles at 12 miles per hour on a bike whose wheels are of diameter 0·7 metre.
How many times does each wheel go round in 1 minute?

To answer this question you need to know that
    1 mile per hour = 0·447 metres per second.